Laura O'Brien is a Partner and Head of the Protest and Public Order Team at Hodge Jones and Allen, one of the leading firms in protest law. Laura is a solicitor with Higher Rights of audience who represents clients in the Magistrates Court, Crown Court and Court of Appeal. Laura is a keen trial advocate and has acted in some of the key protest cases over the last five years including the trial and subsequent appeal arising from the pulling down of the statue of Edward Colston in Bristol, the key protest sentencing cases *R v Trowland* and *R v Hallam*. Laura regularly gives training and provides briefings on protest law.

A Practical Guide to Sentencing in Protest Cases

A Practical Guide to Sentencing in Protest Cases

Laura O'Brien

Partner and Head of the Protest and Public Order Team,
Hodge Jones and Allen

Law Brief Publishing

Published 2025 by Law Brief Publishing, an imprint of Law Brief Publishing Ltd
30 The Parks
Minehead
Somerset
TA24 8BT

www.lawbriefpublishing.com

Paperback: 978-1-916698-89-5

This book is dedicated to Rosa:

to my Rosa, to the Rosa's of history

and to the Rosa's of the future.

PREFACE

This book is written at a time when unprecedented numbers of peaceful protestors are having their liberty taken away. The world is watching.

The proliferation of police powers and criminal offences aimed at the restriction of protestors and their rights means that those representing protestors need to adapt to this increasingly challenging area of law.

The book aims to be a practical and accessible text for legal practitioners. The law outlined in this book is believed to be correct as at 12 May 2025.

Thank you to my colleague Raj Chada without whom I would know nothing about protest law. He is a leading light in protest law and I have been privileged to have been able to work alongside him. Thank you to my clients who have challenged me and taught me.

Laura O'Brien
May 2025

CONTENTS

CHAPTER ONE

INTRODUCTION

While protest is as old as man, the last five years have been significant for protest and the law in the UK.

The last five years have seen a series of judgments dealing with the approach to the right to protest in the context of criminal trials. We have seen the creation of new offences and powers specifically targeted at protest, increased sentencing powers, the use of existing powers used in a way we have not seen before and unprecedented custodial sentences imposed for peaceful protest. We have seen the increased use of civil injunctions to prevent peaceful protest.

Sentencing in protest cases is taking place within the context of shifting legal principles and a decreasing tolerance for direct action and disruptive protest.

This book aims to set out the legal framework and practical considerations for sentencing in protest cases.

CHAPTER TWO

WHAT IS PROTEST?

Protest is the expression or demonstration of dissent or objection. Protest has existed for as long as humans have held opinions and power over each other. It has accompanied every great change in history.

Talking of nonviolent direct action, Martin Luther King (in *Why We Can't* Wait, 1964) said:

> Nonviolence is a powerful and just weapon. It is a weapon unique in history, which cuts without wounding and ennobles the man who wields it. It is a sword that heals.

As protest has been met through history with intimidation, violence and restriction, the law has developed to give it protection and to set the limits of that protection.

2.1 The European Convention on Human Rights

The European Convention on Human Rights was adopted by the Council of Europe in 1950 and came into force in 1953. The Human Rights Act 1998 gave effect in the UK to the rights and freedoms protected under the European Convention on Human Rights.

The right to protest is protected by articles 9, 10 and 11 of the European Convention of Human Rights, although articles 10 and 11 are cited most often in the caselaw. As article 11 is to be interpreted in light of article 10, said to constitute the *lex generalis*, whether arguments refer to article 10 or article 11 is largely immaterial (see *DPP v Ziegler* [2021] UKSC 23 at para 61). In simple terms, freedom of assembly is generally exercised in furtherance of freedom of expression.

The rights under articles 9, 10 and 11 are qualified rights: they can be restricted but only where certain circumstances apply.

> ARTICLE 9
>
> Freedom of thought, conscience and religion
>
> 1. Everyone has the right to freedom of thought, conscience and religion; this right includes freedom to change his religion or belief and freedom, either alone or in community with others and in public or private, to manifest his religion or belief, in worship, teaching, practice and observance.
>
> 2. Freedom to manifest one's religion or beliefs **shall be subject only to such limitations as are prescribed by law and are necessary in a democratic society in the interests of public safety, for the protection of public order, health or morals, or for the protection of the rights and freedoms of others.**
>
> ARTICLE 10
>
> Freedom of expression
>
> 1. Everyone has the right to freedom of expression. This right shall include freedom to hold opinions and to receive and impart information and ideas without interference by public authority and regardless of frontiers. This Article shall not prevent States from requiring the licensing of broadcasting, television or cinema enterprises.
>
> 2. The exercise of these freedoms, since it carries with it duties and responsibilities, **may be subject to such formalities,**

> **conditions, restrictions or penalties as are prescribed by law and are necessary in a democratic society, in the interests of national security, territorial integrity or public safety, for the prevention of disorder or crime, for the protection of health or morals, for the protection of the reputation or rights of others, for preventing the disclosure of information received in confidence, or for maintaining the authority and impartiality of the judiciary.**
>
> ARTICLE 11
>
> Freedom of assembly and association
>
> 1. Everyone has the right to freedom of peaceful assembly and to freedom of association with others, including the right to form and to join trade unions for the protection of his interests.
>
> 2. **No restrictions shall be placed on the exercise of these rights other than such as are prescribed by law and are necessary in a democratic society in the interests of national security or public safety, for the prevention of disorder or crime, for the protection of health or morals or for the protection of the rights and freedoms of others.** This Article shall not prevent the imposition of lawful restrictions on the exercise of these rights by members of the armed forces, of the police or of the administration of the State.

Freedom of expression under article 10 doesn't just protect speech or writing, but also direct action protests. The European Court of Human Rights stated in *Taranenko v Russia* (Application No 19554/05) (at paragraph 70):

> The Court has previously held that protests can constitute expressions of opinion within the meaning of Article 10. Thus,

> protests against hunting involving physical disruption of the hunt or a protest against the extension of a motorway involving a forcible entry into the construction site and climbing into the trees to be felled and onto machinery in order to impede the construction works were found to constitute expressions of opinion protected by Article 10 (see *Steel and Others v. the United Kingdom*, 23 September 1998, § 92, *Reports of Judgments and Decisions* 1998-VII, and *Hashman and Harrup v. the United Kingdom* [GC], no. 25594/94, § 28, ECHR 1999-VIII).

It is worth pausing, before turning to the legal principles surrounding these rights, to consider why they are held as human rights. As the European Court of Human Rights states in *Handyside v United Kingdom* (Application No 5493/72) at paragraph 49, referring to the principles characterising a democratic society:

> Freedom of expression constitutes one of the essential foundations of such a society, one of the basic conditions for its progress and for the development of every man. Subject to paragraph 2 of Article 10 (art. 10-2), it is applicable not only to "information" or "ideas" that are favourably received or regarded as inoffensive or as a matter of indifference, but also to those that offend, shock or disturb the State or any sector of the population. Such are the demands of that pluralism, tolerance and broadmindedness without which there is no "democratic society". This means, amongst other things, that every "formality", "condition", "restriction" or "penalty" imposed in this sphere must be proportionate to the legitimate aim pursued.

The test of necessity in a democratic society requires the Court to determine whether the "interference" complained of corresponded to a "pressing social need", whether it was proportionate to the legitimate aim pursued and whether the reasons given by the national authorities to justify it were relevant and sufficient (*Taranenko v Russia* at para 74).

When assessing whether a restriction on the Convention is necessary in a democratic society, the following set of sub-questions apply:

> (1) Is the aim sufficiently important to justify interference with a fundamental right?
>
> (2) Is there a rational connection between the means chosen and the aim in view?
>
> (3) Are there less restrictive alternative means available to achieve that aim?
>
> (4) Is there a fair balance between the rights of the individual and the general interest of the community, including the rights of others?

As identified by the Divisional Court in *DPP v Ziegler* [2019] EWHC 71 (Admin), in practice it will be last of these questions which will be of crucial importance, whether the restriction strikes the balance between competing rights.

It may be that conduct by protestors will fall outside the protection of articles 9, 10 and 11. As confirmed by Lord Reed in *Reference by the Attorney General for Northern Ireland – Abortion Services (Safe Access Zones) (Northern Ireland) Bill* [2022] UKSC 32 ('*AGNI*') at paragraph 54:

> The conduct in question will fall outside the scope of those articles altogether if it involves **violent intentions, or incites violence, or otherwise rejects the foundations of a democratic society** (*Kudrevičius*, para 92), or if article 17 of the

> Convention applies (article 17 provides that the Convention does not confer any right on a person to engage in any activity or perform any act aimed at the destruction of any of the rights and freedoms set out in the Convention or at their limitation to a greater extent than is provided in the Convention).

The individual facts of the case and the conduct of the offender will need to be considered carefully before making any concession that conduct falls outside the protection of articles 9, 10 and 11.

In *Primov v Russia* (Application No 17391/06) the European Court of Human Rights stated (at paragraph 155) that:

> Article 11 does not cover demonstrations where the organisers and participants have violent intentions ... However, an individual does not cease to enjoy the right to peaceful assembly as a result of sporadic violence or other punishable acts committed by others in the course of the demonstration if the individual in question remains peaceful in his or her own intentions or behaviour...

The Supreme Court in *Ziegler* gave a salient reminder that "a protest is peaceful even though it may annoy or cause offence to the persons opposed to the ideas or claims that the protest is seeking to promote" (para 69).

2.2 Sentence as a restriction on the right to protest

Restrictions on articles 9, 10 and 11 can arise at different stages and in different forms. The Supreme Court in *Ziegler* stated:

> In *Kudrevičius v Lithuania* (2016) 62 EHRR 34, para 100 the European Court of Human Rights ("ECtHR") stated that "The term 'restrictions' in article 11(2) must be interpreted as

> including both measures taken before or during a gathering and those, such as **punitive measures, taken afterwards**" so that it accepted at para 101 "that the applicants' conviction for their participation in the demonstrations at issue amounted to an interference with their right to freedom of peaceful assembly". **Arrest, prosecution, conviction, and sentence are all "restrictions" within both articles.** Different considerations may apply to the proportionality of each of those restrictions. (emphasis added)

Conviction and sentence are distinct restrictions requiring distinct assessments of proportionality.

Following a string of cases addressing reliance on Convention rights in criminal trials, we know that even where the rights are engaged (where the conduct is capable of being protected by the Convention rights), the Court is not necessarily required to undertake a proportionality assessment or consider those rights in deciding the case against the defendant at trial.

In *AGNI*, the Supreme Court outlined the correct approach where a defendant relies on articles 9, 10 or 11 as a defence to a protest-related offence (para 54 to 59). The Court sets out set of questions:

1. Are the rights engaged? As set out earlier in this chapter, non-peaceful conduct will fall outside the protection of these rights (para 54).

2. If engaged, is the offence one where the ingredients of the offence themselves strike the proportionality balance, so that if the ingredients are made out, and the defendant is convicted, there can have been no breach of his or her Convention rights? If the offence is so defined as to ensure that any conviction will meet the requirements of proportionality, the court does not

have to go through the process of verifying that a conviction would be proportionate on the facts of every individual case (para 55).

3. Where the conduct in question falls within the scope of articles 9, 10 or 11, and proof of the ingredients of the offence does not in itself ensure the proportionality of a conviction, the question is then whether there is a means by which the proportionality of a conviction can be ensured. A defence of lawful or reasonable excuse may provide a route by which a proportionality assessment can be carried out (see *Ziegler*).

4. If interpretation in accordance with section 3 cannot resolve the incompatibility, then the court must give effect to primary legislation notwithstanding the violation of Convention rights: section 6(2) of the Human Rights Act.

Where there is no proportionality assessment at trial, this does not mean that articles 9, 10 and 11 will have no bearing on sentence.

In *R v Trowland* [2023] EWCA Crim 919 (addressed in detail in Chapter 3), lawful exercise of articles 9, 10 and 11 as a reasonable excuse to public nuisance was ruled out as an available defence by the trial Judge at the outset of trial. The Court of Appeal still held articles 10 and 11 were relevant to sentence.

In *R v Hallam* [2025] EWCA Crim 199 (addressed in detail below), in approving *Trowland* the Court of Appeal confirmed conscientious motive and the ECHR remain important factors at sentence even if they are not capable of forming any defence at trial.

This reflects the European jurisprudence. In *Kudrevičius v Lithuania* (Application no. 37553/05) the Grand Chamber stated:

> 146. The nature and severity of the penalties imposed are also factors to be taken into account when assessing the proportionality of an interference in relation to the aim pursued (see *Öztürk v. Turkey* [GC], no. 22479/93, § 70, ECHR 1999-VI; *Osmani and Others*, cited above; and *Gün and Others*, cited above, § 82). Where the sanctions imposed on the demonstrators are criminal in nature, they require particular justification (see *Rai and Evans*, cited above). A peaceful demonstration should not, in principle, be rendered subject to the threat of a criminal sanction (see *Akgöl and Göl v. Turkey*, nos. 28495/06 and 28516/06, § 43, 17 May 2011), and notably to deprivation of liberty (see *Gün and Others*, cited above, § 83). Thus, the Court must examine with particular scrutiny the cases where sanctions imposed by the national authorities for non-violent conduct involve a prison sentence (see *Taranenko*, cited above, § 87).

In finding that the sanction imposed was not disproportionate (a suspended sentence), the Court focused on the minimal impact of the sanction on the Applicants' private and professional lives.

In *Taranenko v Russia*, it was the length of pre-trial detention and exceptional seriousness of the sanctions (three years imprisonment suspended for three years) that lead the Court to conclude there had been a violation of article 10, even though arrest and prosecution were not found to amount to a violation.

See also *DPP v Eastburn* [2023] EWHC 1063 (Admin) where the Divisional Court confirmed there is no requirement on the Court to conduct a standalone proportionality assessment in relation to a charge under section 14 of the Public Order Act 1986. The Divisional Court found that although the Court was not required to undertake an assessment of the proportionality of the conviction, even with the limited interference with the rights and freedoms of others, this would be relevant to sentence.

CHAPTER THREE

ADDRESSING CULPABILITY AND HARM

3.1 General sentencing principles

As will be addressed later in this chapter, the Court of Appeal has confirmed that rights under the European Convention of Human Rights are relevant to sentence, reflecting the European jurisprudence. Consideration of these rights will require a distinct approach to sentencing that will not be seen in other cases. General sentencing principles, however, will still apply and are addressed here.

The purposes of sentencing are now set out in the Sentencing Act 2020. Part 2 to 13 of the Act make up the Sentencing Code.

Where an offender is aged 18 or when convicted, unless mandatory sentences apply or an order is being made under Part 3 of the Mental Health Act 1983, the Court must have regard to the following purposes of sentencing (section 57(2)):

(a) the punishment of offenders,

(b) the reduction of crime (including its reduction by deterrence),

(c) the reform and rehabilitation of offenders,

(d) the protection of the public, and

(e) the making of reparation by offenders to persons affected by their offences.

In *Reconceptualising the effectiveness of sentencing: four perspectives* (published 24 September 2024), the Sentencing Council confirmed that these "purposes are listed without a hierarchy or an indication of when a given purpose might be relevant or not".

Where an offender is aged under 18, in addition to the purposes set out above, the Court must have regard to:

(a) the principle aim of the youth justice system (which is to prevent offending (or re-offending) by persons aged under 18

(b) the welfare of the offender

The court **must** (a) follow any sentencing guidelines which are relevant to the offender's case, and (b) **must**, in exercising any other function relating to the sentencing of offenders, follow any sentencing guidelines which are relevant to the exercise of the function, unless the court is satisfied that it would be **contrary to the interests of justice to do so** (section 59).

Where a court is considering the seriousness of any offence, it must consider—

(a) the offender's culpability in committing the offence, and

(b) any harm which the offence—

    i. caused,

    ii. was intended to cause, or

    iii. might foreseeably have caused.

In *R v Hallam* [2025] EWCA Crim 199, the Court of Appeal confirmed that 'might foreseeably have caused' is an objective test.

The Sentencing Council's *General Guidance: overarching principles* are to be used for offences where there is no offence specific guideline and in conjunction with offence specific guidelines.

The General Guidance states that where there are no offence specific guidelines, in reaching a provisional sentence the court should take account of the following:

1. the statutory maximum sentence (and if appropriate minimum sentence) for the offence;

2. sentencing judgments of the Court of Appeal (Criminal Division) for the offence; and

3. definitive sentencing guidelines for analogous offences.

The *Sentencing offenders with mental disorders, developmental disorders, or neurological impairments* applies when sentencing offenders who at the time of the offence and/or at the time of sentencing have **any mental disorder, neurological impairment or developmental disorder**, such as those listed within Annex A of the Guideline. The fact that an offender has an impairment or disorder should **always be considered** by the court but will not necessarily have an impact on sentencing.

The *Overarching Guidelines on the imposition of community and custodial sentences* are often overlooked and are important to consider, especially where there are arguments about whether a case crosses the custody threshold and where sentences that could be suspended are likely. A few key general points from these guidelines which are worth bearing in mind:

1. A community order must not be imposed unless the offence is 'serious enough to warrant the making of such an order'.

2. Where an offender is being sentenced for a non-imprisonable offence, there is no power to make a community order.

3. Sentencers must consider all available disposals at the time of sentence; even where the threshold for a community sentence has been passed, a fine or discharge may be an appropriate penalty.

4. Sentences should not necessarily escalate from one community order range to the next on each sentencing occasion.

5. A custodial sentence must not be imposed unless the offence or the combination of the offence and one or more offences associated with it was so serious that neither a fine alone nor a community sentence can be justified for the offence. **Passing the custody threshold does not mean that a custodial sentence should be deemed inevitable.** Custody should not be imposed where a community order could provide sufficient restriction on an offender's liberty (by way of punishment) while addressing the rehabilitation of the offender to prevent future crime.

6. For offenders on the cusp of custody, imprisonment should not be imposed where there would be an impact on dependants which would make a custodial sentence disproportionate to achieving the aims of sentencing.

The Overarching Guidelines on the imposition of community and custodial sentences set out the factors to be weighed in considering whether it is possible to suspend the sentence in the table below.

Factors indicating that it would not be appropriate to suspend a custodial sentence	**Factors indicating that it may be appropriate to suspend a custodial sentence**
Offender presents a risk/danger to the public	Realistic prospect of rehabilitation
Appropriate punishment can only be achieved by immediate custody	Strong personal mitigation
History of poor compliance with court orders	Immediate custody will result in significant harmful impact upon others

Realistic prospect of rehabilitation can often be a live issue in protest cases. Protest cases arise where people are involved in conduct because of their beliefs. For that reason the conscientious motivations of the offender are taken into account (as will be dealt with in more detail later in this chapter).

Someone who believes that a genocide is being carried out in Gaza, that there is institutional racism in the UK or that the Government is failing to do enough to address the climate crisis is very unlikely to abandon those beliefs and it would not be appropriate or compliant with their rights under the European Convention on Human Rights for the court to expect them to do so.

It is the conduct and not the belief that the offender is being sentenced for. The focus should therefore be on the prospect of them not being involved in **criminal** conduct in the future.

In *R v Hallam* the Court of Appeal rejected an argument that the sentencing Judge had effectively required the Defendants to disavow Just Stop Oil to avoid immediate custody, highlighting his comment that their continued commitment to their cause was not in itself objectionable.

Sentencing of children and young people

Sentencing for offenders under 18 is a specialist subject in itself and this book can only touch on it briefly.

Anyone dealing with the sentence of an offender the age of 18 should consider the checklist set out by the Court of Appeal in *R v ZA* [2023] EWCA Crim 596:

> (1) Court listing should ensure that there is **sufficient time** for the judge, even if that judge heard the trial and knows the case well, to read and consider all reports and to prepare sentencing remarks in age-appropriate language.
>
> (2) Consideration should be given to **listing separately, and as a priority, the sentence of any child(ren) or young person(s)** jointly convicted with adult co-defendants.
>
> (3) The courtroom should be set up and arranged to ensure that the child or young person to be sentenced is treated appropriately, namely as a **vulnerable defendant entitled to proper support**. So far as possible the judge should be seated on a level with the child or young person, and the latter should be able to sit near to counsel, with parental or other support seated next to them (see further below).
>
> (4) Counsel must expect to submit **full sentencing notes identifying all relevant Sentencing Council Guidelines, in**

particular any youth-specific guideline(s), addressing material considerations in an individualistic way for each defendant separately (if more than one young defendant is to be sentenced). Where an individualistic approach is mandated, as it is for a child or young person, a note which addresses all defendants compendiously risks missing important distinctions. These notes should be uploaded well in advance of the sentencing hearing.

(5) The contents of the Youth Justice Service pre-sentence report and any medical/psychiatric/psychological reports will be key. Courts should consider these reports bearing in mind the general principles at section 1 of the overarching youth guideline, together with any youth-specific offence guideline, carefully working through each.

(6) In general it will not be helpful to go straight to paragraph 6.46 of the overarching youth guideline without having first directed the court to general principles canvassed earlier in that guideline, as well as to any youth-specific guideline. **The stepped approach in the overarching youth guideline and any youth-specific offence guideline should be followed.** Working through the guideline(s) in this way will enable the court to arrive at the most appropriate sentence for the particular child or young person, bearing in mind their individual circumstances together with the dual aims of youth sentencing.

(7) If the court considers that the **offence(s) is(are) so serious as to pass the custody threshold, the court must consider whether a YRO with ISS can be imposed instead.** If it cannot, then the court must explain why.

Where an offender turns 18 after proceedings have begun, the Court has a discretion to remit the case to the Magistrates Court (section 27 of the Sentencing Code). The Court has the discretion to impose a youth sentence even where an offender has turned 18 during the course of proceedings. An offender who has turned 18 after the commission of an offence but before the commencement of proceedings will be dealt with as an adult.

Where dealing with offenders who have passed the age threshold of 18 in the time between commission of the offence and sentence, the case of *R v Ahmed & others* [2023] EWCA Crim 281 will apply. In dealing with a number of appeals relating to sentences for sexual offending, the Court of Appeal set out the following principles:

> i) Whatever may be the offender's age at the time of conviction and sentence, **the Children guideline is relevant and must be followed unless the court is satisfied that it would be contrary to the interests of justice to do so.**
>
> ii) **The court must have regard to (though is not necessarily restricted by: see (v) below) the maximum sentence which was available in the case of the offender at or shortly after the time of his offending.** Depending on the nature of the offending and the age of the offender, that maximum may be (a) the same as would have applied to an adult offender; (b) limited by statutory provisions setting a different maximum for an offender who had not attained a particular age; or (c) limited by statutory provisions restricting the availability of different types or lengths of custodial sentence according to the age of the offender.
>
> iii) The court must take as its starting point the **sentence which it considers was likely to have been imposed if the child offender had been sentenced shortly after the offence.**

iv) If in all the circumstances of the case the child offender could not in law have been sentenced (at the time of his offending) to any form of custody, then no custodial sentence may be imposed.

v) Where some form of custody was available, **the court is not necessarily bound by the maximum applicable to the child offender.** The court should, however, only exceed that maximum where there is good reason to do so. In this regard, the mere fact that the offender has now attained adulthood is not in itself a good reason. We would add that we find it very difficult to think of circumstances in which a good reason could properly be found, and we respectfully doubt the decision in Forbes in this respect. However, the point was not specifically argued before us, and a decision about it must therefore await a case in which it is directly raised.

vi) The starting point taken in accordance with (iii) above will not necessarily be the end point. **Subsequent events may enable the court to be sure that the culpability of the child offender was higher, or lower, than would likely have been apparent at the time of the offending.** They may show that an offence was not, as it might have seemed at the time, an isolated lapse by a child, but rather a part of a continuing course of conduct. The passage of time may enable the court to be sure that the harm caused by the offending was greater than would likely have been apparent at that time. Because the court is sentencing an adult, it must have regard to the purposes of sentencing set out in section 57 of the Sentencing Code. In each case, the issue for the court to resolve will be whether there is good reason to impose on the adult a sentence more severe than he would have been likely to have received if he had been sentenced soon after the offence as a child.

In the context of protest, the involvement of the offender in further criminal conduct or lack thereof in the period between the offence and sentence, including offending which indicates the offender has an organisational role, is likely to be highly relevant.

When looking at what the sentence would have been had the offender been sentenced close in time to the commission of the offence, careful analysis of the adult equivalent of a youth sentence will need to be undertaken. An adult community order is not the direct equivalent of a referral order and consideration should be given to a conditional discharge for adult offenders who would have received a referral order had they been sentenced closer in time to the offence. Although they are rarely imposed, absolute discharges remain a valid sentencing option and should not be overlooked. There will still be cases where an absolute discharge is arguably the just and proportionate response.

Age remains a relevant factor for young people, even when offending occurs after the age of 18. In *R v Clarke* [2018] EWCA Crim 185 the then Lord Chief Justice stated (at paragraph 5):

> Reaching the age of 18 has many legal consequences, but it does not present a cliff edge for the purposes of sentencing. So much has long been clear. The discussion in *R v Peters* [2005] EWCA Crim 605, [2005] 2 Cr App R(S) 101 is an example of its application: See paras [10]-[12]. Full maturity and all the attributes of adulthood are not magically conferred on young people on their 18th birthdays. Experience of life reflected in scientific research (e.g. The Age of Adolescence: thelancet.com/child-adolescent; 17 January 2018) is that young people continue to mature, albeit at different rates, for some time beyond their 18th birthdays. The youth and maturity of an offender will be factors that inform any sentencing decision, even if an offender has passed his or her 18th birthday.

It is often the case that offences committed in the course of a protest will involve multiple defendants. It is important that the individuals circumstances of a defendant do not get overlooked.

3.2 Conscientious motives

It has long been recognised that where someone commits a criminal offence as a result of conscientious motives, this should be reflected in sentencing.

In *R v Jones (Margaret)* [2006] UKHL 16 [2007] 1 AC 136 Lord Hoffmann (at para 89) referred to sentences being imposed which took into account the conscientious motives of the protestors:

> "My Lords, civil disobedience on conscientious grounds has a long and honourable history in this country. People who break the law to affirm their belief in the injustice of a law or government action are sometimes vindicated by history. The suffragettes are an example which comes immediately to mind. It is the mark of a civilised community that it can accommodate protests and demonstrations of this kind. But there are conventions which are generally accepted by the law-breakers on one side and the law-enforcers on the other. The protesters behave with a sense of proportion and do not cause excessive damage or inconvenience. And they vouch the sincerity of their beliefs by accepting the penalties imposed by the law. The police and prosecutors, on the other hand, behave with restraint and the magistrates impose sentences which take the conscientious motives of the protesters into account. The conditional discharges ordered by the magistrates in the cases which came before them exemplifies their sensitivity to these conventions."

In *R v Roberts & Others* [2018] EWCA Crim 2739 the Court stated (at para 32) the Court held that crimes committed in the course of peaceful protest does not generally impute high levels of culpability:

> "...it is well established that committing crimes, at least non-violent crimes, in the course of peaceful protest does not generally impute high levels of culpability."

> "Paragraph 89 [of Lord Hoffmann's judgment in *R v Jones*] echoes the understanding that the conscientious motives of protestors <u>will be taken into account when they are sentenced for their offences</u> but that there is in essence a bargain or mutual understanding operating in such cases. A sense of proportion on the part of the offenders in avoiding excessive damage or inconvenience is matched by a relatively benign approach to sentencing. When sentencing an offender, <u>the value of the right to freedom of expression finds its voice in the approach to sentencing</u>." (at [34], emphasis added)

In *Cuadrilla Bowland v Persons Unknown* [2020] EWCA Civ 9 [2020] 4 W.L.R. 29 (at para 89) the Court addressed the moral difference between those who act for conscientious motives and ordinary law-breakers:

> "It seems to me that there are at <u>least three reasons for showing greater clemency in response to such acts of civil disobedience than in dealing with other disobedience of the law</u>. <u>First</u>, by adhering to the conditions mentioned, a person who engages in acts of civil disobedience establishes <u>a moral difference</u> between herself and ordinary law-breakers which it is right to take into account in determining what punishment is deserved. <u>Second</u>, by reason of that difference and the fact that such <u>a protestor is generally—apart from their protest activity—a law-abiding citizen</u>, there is reason to expect that

> less severe punishment is necessary to deter such a person from further law-breaking. Third, part of the purpose of imposing sanctions, whether for a criminal offence or for intentional breach of an injunction, is to engage in a dialogue with the defendant so that he or she appreciates the reasons why in a democratic society it is the duty of responsible citizens to obey the law and respect the rights of others, even where the law or other people's lawful activities are contrary to the protestor's own moral convictions. Such a dialogue is more likely to be effective where authorities (including judicial authorities) show restraint in anticipation that the defendant will respond by desisting from further breaches. This is part of what I believe Lord Burnett CJ meant in the *Roberts* case at para 34 (quoted above) when he referred to "a bargain or mutual understanding operating in such cases".

Deterrent sentences have become a live issue in protest cases. In *Cuadrilla* the Court refers to deterring the individual from further law-breaking. Assessing how best to achieve deterrence on an individual basis requires a careful assessment of an individual's personal circumstances and offending history.

But deterrent sentencing can also focus on the pressing social need to deter certain types of offending. There is an obvious tension between sentences designed to deter certain types of direct action protest and often specific protest movements and the protections afforded to freedom of expression and freedom of assembly.

The concept of a 'chilling effect' is well established in the caselaw of the European Court of Human Rights. In *The Concept of chilling effect: it's untapped potential to better protect democracy, the rule of law, and fundamental rights in the EU*, Open Society, European Policy Institute (March 2021) the long established principle of a 'chilling effect' was addressed:

> From a legal point of view, chilling effect may be defined as the negative effect any state action has on natural and/or legal persons, and which results in pre-emptively dissuading them from exercising their rights or fulfilling their professional obligations, for fear of being subject to formal state proceedings which could lead to sanctions or informal consequences such as threats, attacks or smear campaigns. State action is understood in this context as any measure, practice or omission by public authorities which may deter natural and/or legal persons from exercising any of the rights provided to them under national, European and/or international law, or may discourage the potential fulfilment of one's professional obligations (as in the case of judges, prosecutors and lawyers, for instance).

In *Navalny v. Russia* (Application no. 76204/11), the Court held that the suppression of a march, the Applicant's arrest and subsequent conviction were all disproportionate interferences with the Applicant's rights under articles 10 and 11:

> 73. The Court has found above that the measures applied to the applicants were not proportionate to the legitimate aim pursued. It further notes that the police and the courts expressly acknowledged that, ultimately, the applicants had been punished for holding a spontaneous peaceful demonstration and chanting anti-government slogans, acts protected by Articles 10 and 11 of the Convention. The courts devoted no effort to balancing the applicants' legitimate interests against any damage this could cause to other public or private interests. The dispersal of the perceived march, the arrest and the ensuing administrative conviction of the applicants could not but have the effect of discouraging them from participating in protest rallies or indeed from engaging actively in opposition politics.

> 74. Undoubtedly, those measures had a serious potential also to deter other opposition supporters and the public at large from attending demonstrations and, more generally, from participating in open political debate. The chilling effect of those sanctions was further amplified by the fact that they targeted well-known public figures, whose deprivation of liberty was bound to attract broad media coverage.

While reduction in crime including through deterrence is a purpose of sentencing, sanctions which discourage the exercise of freedom of conscience, freedom of expression and freedom of assembly, not just by the individual cannot be justified.

3.3 R v Trowland

The key authority on sentencing in protest cases is *R v Trowland* [2023] EWCA Crim 919. A judgment handed by Lady Justice Carr shortly before taking on her role as Lady Chief Justice.

In the early hours of 17 October 2022 the Appellants exited a vehicle on the Queen Elizabeth II (QEII) Bridge, suspended themselves on wires attached to the two sides of the bridge, over the roadway, and remained there for approximately 36 hours.

Both were charged with statutory public nuisance, an offence that had only existed for a number of months at the time, having been introduced by section 78 of the Police, Crime, Sentencing and Courts Act 2022. Both were remanded in custody awaiting trial and were convicted on 4 April 2023.

On 21 of April 2023 the Appellants were sentenced to three years in the case of Mr Trowland and two years and seven months in the case of Mr Decker.

At trial, the prosecution had relied on a significant volume of evidence in relation to the impact of the protest. It included data in relation to the number of cars impacted, the economic impact on businesses and testimony from civilian witnesses who had been impacted by the disruption. The evidence given by the Appellants at trial featured heavily in the sentencing remarks and in the Court of Appeal judgment.

The sentencing Judge made specific reference to their attitude at trial and rejected the Appellants' apologies, describing them as hollow and self-serving. The Judge focused on the previous convictions of both defendants.

The Judge referenced the maximum sentence of 10 years imprisonment which allow for a range of sentences that were fact specific and cater for the many different ways in which the offence could be committed.

The Judge cited the various purposes of sentencing and stated the two he had very much in mind were punishment and the reduction of crime by deterrence. The Judge referred to the disproportionate nature of the offending and described the aim of the Appellants as being to achieve maximum publicity by causing maximum disruption by means of a spectacular protest event.

The Judge found both culpability and harm to be high. The statutory aggravating features were the relevant previous convictions of the Appellants and the fact that the offences were committed whilst on bail which was regarded as being a serious aggravating feature. The Judge found that Mr Trowland played a leading role and took a starting point of four years imprisonment which was reduced to 3 years to reflect this was a matter of conscience. For Mr Decker the judge drew some distinction between his position and that of Mr Trowland and took a starting point of three years and six months in prison. This was reduced at two years and seven months to reflect the fact this was a matter of conscience.

On the 31st of July 2023 the court of appeal dismissed their appeal against sentence. The sentences were described as severe but not held to be manifestly excessive.

The following principles can be taken from the judgment:

a. Paragraph 48:

    i. The seriousness of the offence is to be assessed by considering the culpability of the offender and the harm caused by the offending (see s. 63 of the Sentencing Act 2020).

    ii. The court must also consider which of the five purposes of sentencing identified in s.57 of the Sentencing Act 2020, namely punishment, reduction of crime (including its reduction by deterrence), reform and rehabilitation, public protection and the making of reparation, it is seeking to achieve through the sentence that is to be imposed.

    iii. Once a provisional sentence is arrived at, the court takes into account relevant aggravating and mitigating features. Other considerations, such as totality, may be engaged under the stepped approach set out in the Sentencing Council's General Guideline: Overarching Principles.

    iv. Custodial sentences must be what is, in the opinion of the court, the shortest term commensurate with the seriousness of the offence (see s. 231(2) of the Sentencing Act 2020).

b. Paragraph 49:

   i. The (qualified) rights to freedom of expression and assembly under Articles 10 and 11 are relevant to sentence.

   ii. Particular caution is to be exercised in imposing a custodial sentence in nonviolent protest cases.

   iii. Determination of the proportionality of an interference with ECHR rights is a fact-specific enquiry which requires the evaluation of the circumstances in the individual case. It is a flexible notion, which depends on fair and objective judicial assessment; there are no rigid rules to be applied.

c. Paragraph 50:

   i. A conscientious motive on the part of protesters may be a relevant consideration, in particular where the offender is a law-abiding citizen apart from their protest activities. In such cases, a lesser sanction may be appropriate: a sense of proportion on the part of the offender in avoiding excessive damage or inconvenience may be matched by a relatively benign approach to sentencing.

   ii. The court may temper the sanction imposed because there is a realistic prospect that it will deter further law-breaking and encourage the offender to appreciate why in a democratic society it is the duty of responsible citizens to obey the law and respect the rights of others, even where the law is contrary to the protestors' own moral convictions.

iii. The more disproportionate or extreme the action taken by the protester, the less obvious is the justification for reduced culpability and more lenient sentencing.

iv. Conscientious motivation did not preclude a finding that any appellant's culpability was still high.

d. Paragraph 51:

i. Whether or not a sentence of immediate custody for this type of offending is warranted, and if so what length of sentence is appropriate, will be highly fact sensitive, set in the context of the relevant legislative and sentencing regime identified above.

e. Paragraph 55:

i. Conscientious motivation was a factor most logically relevant to the assessment of culpability, as opposed to general mitigation

The Court of Appeal rejected the argument that the over-reliance on deterrence risks having a 'chilling effect' on freedom of expression, stating (at paragraph 90):

> The sentences should not be seen as having a "chilling effect" on the right to peaceful protest or to assembly more generally; deterrence and "chilling effect" are not the same. This protest was of a wholly different nature and scale to the many nonviolent protests of conscientious activists up and down the country exercising their rights to freedom of expression and assembly on a daily basis.

Simply citing deterrence however cannot safeguard a sentence which is so severe as to discourage the lawful exercise of Convention rights. Sentences must be just and proportionate whether they involve conscientious motives or not but proportionality takes on an enhanced meaning when offending is a matter of conscience.

3.4 R v Hallam

In *R v Hallam & others* [2025] EWCA Crim 199, in which judgment was handed down on 7 March 2025, the Court of Appeal considered appeals against sentence arising in four different cases. Judgment was again handed down by Lady Justice Carr who also presided over the Court in *Trowland.*

Hallam and others

Roger Hallam, Lucia Whittaker De Abreu, Daniel Shaw, Louise Lancaster and Cressida Gethin were all convicted after trial of conspiracy to cause a public nuisance. This case arose from a Zoom call in which plans were discussed for Just Stop Oil protestors to go onto gantries over the M25 in November 2022. A plan which resulted in protests on gantries over the M25 on four consecutive days. Roger Hallam was sentenced to five years imprisonment and the remaining Appellants were sentenced to four years imprisonment. On appeal, Roger Hallam's sentence was reduced to one of four years imprisonment, Daniel Shaw and Louise Lancaster's sentences were reduced to three years and Lucia Whittaker De Abreu and Cressida Gethin's were reduced to 30 months.

The Court of Appeal endorsed the sentencing Judge's view that the offending in this case was worse than in *Trowland* with the intended effect being worse and the period of disruption longer.

Cressida Gethin was only 20 years old at the time of the offence. In reducing her sentence, the Court of Appeal endorsed the principles in *Clarke* (98): "Intelligence and educational attainment are not the same as maturity. Consideration of the possible relevance of immaturity is necessary even in the case of a young adult who has passed the age at which the Guideline on Sentencing Children and Young People applies."

Delap and others

Gaie Delap, Paul Sousek, Theresa Higginson, Paul Bell and George Simonson all pleaded guilty shortly before trial to causing a public nuisance by going onto gantries over the M25 in November 2022. Save for Gaie Delap's sentence which was reduced to reflect time spent on restrictive bail conditions, the appeals were refused.

Bennett and others

Chris Bennett, Dr Larch Maxey, Samuel Johnson and Joe Howlett were all convicted after trial of conspiracy to cause a public nuisance after digging and occupying a tunnel under a reading leading to the Navigator Oil Terminal in Essex. Dr Maxey was sentenced to three years imprisonment, Chris Bennett and Samuel Johnson to 18 months imprisonment and Joe Howlett to 15 months imprisonment. All appeals were refused.

Plummer and Holland

Phoebe Plummer and Anna Holland were convicted after trial having thrown tomato soup at one of a number of Vincent Van Gough's "Sunflowers" which was framed behind protective glass at the National Gallery. No damage was done to the painting itself but there was damage to the frame. Phoebe Plummer was sentenced to 24 months immediate custody and Anna Holland to 20 months immediate custody. Both appeals were refused.

Principles from *R v Hallam*

At the outset of the judgment the Lady Justice distilled the central points of principle to the following:

i. The exercise of sentencing in cases of non-violent protests is to be carried out in accordance with normal sentencing principles, including those contained in ss. 57, 63 and 231(2) of the Sentencing Act 2020.

ii. The correct approach to issues that may arise when sentencing in cases of nonviolent protests, such as conscientious motivation and deterrence, was considered authoritatively in *R v Trowland* [2023] EWCA Crim 919; [2024] 1 WLR 1164 (*Trowland*).

iii. The sentencing exercise in cases of non-violent protest should not be overcomplicated because of the engagement of the European Convention of Human Rights (ECHR). Whether or not Articles 10 and/or 11 of the ECHR (Article 10; Article 11) are engaged should be simple; if engaged, the court then has to carry out what should be a straightforward proportionality exercise. There should be no need to make extensive reference to domestic or international authorities.

The common law and the ECHR are in step. If the common law principles in *Trowland* are applied properly, the defendant's ECHR rights should be observed.

iv. References to the sentencing outcomes in different cases are unlikely to be helpful, since each case will turn on its own facts. It can also be dangerous. The term of three years imposed in *Trowland* was not a tariff of any sort. Indeed, whilst upheld on appeal, it was held to be severe (and arguably manifestly excessive). An approach that treats a three-year term for offending similar to that in *Trowland* as a benchmark risks undesirable and unwarranted sentence inflation.

Further points arise through the response to each ground of appeal:

i. A sentencing judge is not obliged to specify an amount by which they have reduced a custodial term to reflect a defendant's conscientious motivation. As a general proposition, a sentencing judge is not obliged to attribute specific percentage values or figures to individual factors which have been taken into account in the sentencing exercise: see for example *R v Ratcliffe* [2024] EWCA Crim 1498 at [81]. That includes not only aggravating and mitigating factors, but also factors, such as conscientious motivation, going to the assessment of culpability. There is no parallel to be drawn with the approach to discounts for guilty pleas, for which a quantified reduction in sentence is made at a discrete stage in the sentencing process (26).

ii. The Court noted that the appellants' message in these cases constituted "political speech", to which particular respect is afforded: it involved a call for a change in the law. There were ways in which the appellants could have communicated that message without trespassing and without committing a criminal offence. But the fact that they committed a trespass and a criminal offence in communicating that message did not mean that their activity ceased to be an expression of their views (28).

iii. Articles 10 and 11 did not confer on the appellants a right of entry to private property: see *Appleby v United Kingdom* (2003) Application No. 44306/98. Moreover, disrupting traffic has been held not to be at the core of Articles 10 and 11: see *Kudrevičius v Lithuania* (2015) 62 E.H.R.R. 34, at 91. But neither of these cases (nor any other) supported the contention that a protester who commits an act of trespass thereby automatically loses their rights under Article 10 or 11 altogether.

iv. The Judge in the Sunflowers case was right to conclude that Article 10 and 11 were not engaged if the actions were violent/non-peaceful but was not correct to hold that they were also not engaged if the damage was significant (*Attorney General's Reference (No 1 of 2022*) [2022] EWCA Crim 1259; [2023] KB 37 (Colston). The Court of Appeal referred to the case of *Murat Vural v Turkey* (2014) Application No. 9540/07 in which the applicant poured paint on five public statutes of Kemal Atatűrk in finding in relation to Phoebe Plummer and Anna Holland: "While shocking, their actions were not violent."

v. In relation to the assessment of harm, the question of harm that 'might foreseeably have been caused' is an objective rather than subjective one (182).

While it is without question positive that the judgment reinforces the significance of conscientious motive and the Convention rights at sentencing, doing so while upholding significant custodial sentences sanctions the ongoing imprisonment of peaceful protestors.

At sentence it will be important to focus on the specific facts of the case, to really engage with the general sentencing principles and to warn the Court against using the sentences in *Trowland* or indeed *Hallam* as any sort of benchmark.

3.5 Deterrent sentences

Deterrence has been cited in justifying a number of non-violent protestors being given immediate custodial sentences.

One of the purposes of sentencing is "the reduction of crime (including its reduction by deterrence)" although deterrence is not defined in the Sentencing Code. In *Trowland* the Court of Appeal confirmed that deterrence to the wider public, not just the protestors themselves may be a highly relevant consideration. At paragraph 86 the Court said: "It can be said that the principle of deterrence is of both particular relevance and importance in the context of a pressing social need to protect the public and to prevent social unrest arising from escalating illegal activity."

In April 2025 Just Stop Oil announced their campaign would come to an end. It will be as relevant to highlight a reducing social need for deterrence as it will be to highlight a pressing social need.

Even where deterrence is to form a part of considerations at sentencing, careful consideration needs to be given to how it is reflected in sentencing.

In *Reconceptualising the effectiveness of sentencing: four perspectives* (published 24 September 2024), the Sentencing Council said:

> There is not robust empirical evidence to suggest that, in general, more severe sentences provide greater marginal deterrent effects. While this does not mean that the criminal justice system will never deter offending (see the points concerning absolute deterrence and special deterrence above), it does raise important questions about the role of deterrence as a consideration in the sentencing process.

Deterrence can be achieved in different ways and there is no presumption that deterrent sentencing means imposing the most severe form of sanction. Even sentence with deterrence as one of its main aims remains fact specific.

The Sentencing Council cited Bun, M.J.G., Kelaher, R., Sarafidis, V. and Weatherburn, D. (2020) 'Crime, deterrence and punishment revisited', Empirical Economics, 59(5):

> The results of our analysis show that criminal activity is highly responsive to the prospect of arrest and conviction, but much less responsive to the prospect or severity of imprisonment, if at all. This provides support to the idea that the consequences of being arrested and found guilty of a criminal offence include indirect sanctions imposed by society and not just the punishment meted out by the criminal justice system. In particular, a convicted individual may no longer enjoy the same opportunities in the labour market and so the cost of social stigmatization can already be substantial in the event of conviction… This indicates that imprisoning more criminals or imprisoning them for longer, is not as effective [as a deterrent] as increasing the risk of apprehension or conviction once arrested. In other words, criminal activity seems to be

> highly responsive to the prospect of arrest and conviction, but less responsive to the prospect or severity of imprisonment.

Conditional discharges, community orders and suspended sentence all carry the potential for deterrent effect: the prospective of resentence or activation of a suspended sentence may be more effective than an immediate custodial sentence in deterring further offending.

Deterrence should not be conflated with severity or a requirement for imprisonment.

It will also be necessary to consider other factors which may already have a deterrent effect, for example injunctions, undertakings or restraining orders being in place. Many protestors will have been subject to injunctions or entered into undertakings mirroring the terms of an injunction. Where injunctions have been dealt with in the High Court judgments will be published and can be used as evidence in support of mitigation.

3.6 Impact of trial process

In all cases, what happens at trial can have an impact on sentence.

The fact of a trial will of course impact sentence as an offender will not be entitled to any credit for an early guilty plea.

Facts agreed and evidence called will impact on the basis of any sentence. Sentencing Judges are entitled to determine the factual basis of sentence based on the evidence adduced at trial. In *R v Stone* [2011] EWCA Crim 1602 the Court of Appeal stated:

> 15. There is nothing inherently wrong in principle or unfair about a trial judge's expressing his or her own conclusions on the facts, based on the evidence as called, even if the jury has

> not been called upon to make its own findings. However, a trial judge must always exercise great care to ensure that he or she does not appear to go behind the verdicts of a jury and make findings of fact which are inconsistent with those verdicts and the findings the jury was called upon to make. The line may be a fine one…
>
> 18. However, as serious as such an offence is, it must be put in its factual context remembering that the court is not a court of morals.

As seen in the Sunflowers case in *R v Hallam*, the finding of facts at trial may well determine whether the Judge needs to consider the conscientious motive and Convention rights of the Defendant at all. In cases of criminal damage, although there may be no dispute about whether damage was significant or not, there may well be argument over whether it is was 'non-peaceful'. While a jury would not be asked to determine this question, a sentencing Tribunal will have to. How evidence is challenged and presented will need to have in mind the facts which could determine whether the conscientious motives are considered at all at sentencing.

In practice, beyond the facts of the offending, the sentencing Judge may also form a view of the attitude of the offender. What has been seen in recent sentencing exercises in protest cases is the extent to which the sentencing Judge has relied on evidence given at trial and the attitude of the offender to the Court process when passing sentence.

In most protest trials, involvement will not be in dispute and instead the focus will be on whether the conduct was justified and whether it meets the threshold for criminal responsibility. It will be rare for those who have acted out of conscientious motives to disavow their actions completely, even if they regret the impact of their actions on others.

This creates a tension in relation to assessments of remorse and prospect of rehabilitation. If the principles in relation to sentencing those who act as a matter of conscience are not adhered to, there is a risk that offenders are punished further for their motives.

3.7 Terrorist connection

While terrorism legislation is not new, there has been a renewed use of terrorism legislation in the context of protest, particularly in relation to protests against military action in Gaza following the attacks on 7 October 2023. Terrorism is a specialist subject and can only be covered briefly in this book. There is a specific sentencing regime for serious terrorist offences which is not addressed here.

Even where a Defendant is not charged under counter-terrorism legislation, an offence may still be held to have a terrorist connection.

Where an offence has a terrorist connection the Court must treat this as an aggravating factor and must state in open Court that the offence has been treated as aggravated in this way (section 69(2) of the Sentencing Act 2020.

An offence has a terrorist connection if it was committed in the course of an act of terrorism or it was committed for the purpose of terrorism.

Terrorism is defined under section 1 of the Terrorism Act 2000 as the use or threat of action designed to influence the government or an international governmental organisation or to intimidate the public or a section of the public, and the use or threat is made for the purpose of advancing a political, religious racial or ideological cause.

'Action' falling within this definition is action which:

i. involves serious violence against a person,

ii. involves serious damage to property,

iii. endangers a person's life, other than that of the person committing the action,

iv. creates a serious risk to the health or safety of the public or a section of the public, or is designed seriously to interfere with or seriously to disrupt an electronic system

v. involves the use of firearms or explosives

The powers under counter-terrorism legislation are broad and the definitions often very wide. The recent use of this legislation in the context of direct-action protest marks a worrying trend. This is another scenario where the facts at trial could significantly impact the lens through which sentencing is approached.

CHAPTER FOUR

COMMON OFFENCES

A number of key cases and principles are outlined below for offences commonly arising in the context of protests.

4.1 Public nuisance

In *R v Roberts* [2018] EWCA Crim 2739 were convicted of common law public nuisance as part of a demonstration about fracking. The Applicants sat on top of lorries for between two and a half and three days. The Court described substantial disruption being caused to thousands of people. Having found that the custody threshold had not been passed and that a community sentence punitive element would have met the justice of the cases, replaced sentences of 16 and 15 months with conditional discharges due to the time already spent on remand.

In *Smith* [2021] EWCA Crim 1621, the Court of Appeal held that in the absence of an offence specific guideline, it was appropriate to consider definitive guidelines for offences which were similar on the facts. This position is reflected in the *General Guidance: overarching principles.* In cases where a public nuisance is caused by damage, the criminal damage guidelines may be considered.

In *R v Brown* [2022] EWCA Crim 6, the Appellant was convicted of common public nuisance having glued himself to the roof of a plane at London City Airport. The Appellant was found to have intended to cause as much disruption as possible. The Court reduced a sentence of 12 months imprisonment to six months imprisonment before reducing further to four months to reflect Appellant's personal circumstances.

In *R v Trowland* [2023] EWCA Crim 919, the Court of Appeal upheld sentences of three years and two years and seven months for the two Appellants who were convicted after trial of the new statutory public nuisance offence. The Appellants had suspended themselves over the Queen Elizabeth II Bridge for just under two days as part of a Just Stop Oil protest. The disruption caused was described as extreme and their real aim to "achieve maximum publicity by causing maximum disruption by means of a spectacular protest event". Culpability and harm were found to be high and relevant previous convictions and being on bail were seen as serious aggravating features. The Judge took starting points of four years and three years and six months before reducing to reflect that this was a 'matter of conscience'. Although the Court of Appeal did not criticise the reduction given held that the reference to a starting point was technically incorrect as it was a term reserved for a starting point in Sentencing Council Guidelines.

In *R v Hallam* [2025] EWCA Crim 199:

i. A sentence of four years was imposed on appeal on Roger Hallam, co-founder of Extinction Rebellion and Just Stop Oil, for conspiracy to cause a public nuisance which centred around a Zoom planning call in relation to a week of protests on the M25. Two of his co-defendants received sentences on appeal of three years and two received sentences of 30 months.

ii. Sentences ranging from 20 months to 24 months immediate custody were upheld on appeal for climbing gantries over the M25 in November 2022.

iii. Sentences of three years, 18 months and 15 months were upheld on appeal for causing a public nuisance by tunnelling under a road which was occupied for weeks.

4.2 Criminal damage

The maximum sentence for criminal damage is 10 years imprisonment. Criminal damage (other than fire) is an either-way offence but for the purposes of allocation, criminal damage under £5,000 is treated as a summary offence with a maximum sentence of three months' imprisonment.

Where damage is caused to a memorial when the maximum sentence is 10 years imprisonment regardless of the value.

In *R v Hallam* [2025] EWCA Crim 199, the Court of Appeal upheld sentences of 24 months and 20 months immediate custody imposed for criminal damage to Vincent Van Gough's "Sunflowers" at the National Gallery. The Court of Appeal found that the Judge was entitled to find that there was a high degree of culpability due to the level of planning which involved contacting a journalist in advance to maximise the publicity. The offence was aggravated by the fact it was damage to "heritage and / or cultural assets". The judgment however warns against treating specific cases as creating benchmarks and stresses the importance of sentencing turning on the facts of the case. The Court of Appeal did confirm that as the conduct was shocking not violent, Articles 10 and 11 were engaged even though the damage was significant and conscientious motive should still have been considered at sentencing.

4.3 Violent disorder

Although conduct will fall outside the scope of Articles 10 and 11 where it is violent or has violent intentions, public order offences can often arise from otherwise peaceful protests. The fact that a demonstration was attended with peaceful intent and the context of the demonstration may be relevant to sentence.

In *R v Gilmour* [2011] EWCA Crim 2458 the Court upheld a sentence of 16 months imprisonment for an offence of violent disorder arising from the London riots. The Appellant had thrown a bin at a car with members of the Royal Family in it. The Court stated at paragraph 8:

> It is an unavoidable feature of mass disorder that each individual act, whatever might be its character taken on its own, inflames and encourages others to behave similarly, and that the harm done to the public stems from the combined effect of what is done en masse.

In contrast, in *R v Al-Dahi* [2013] EWCA Crim 1267, the Court highlighted the difference in context to *Gilmour*, the Appellant having attended a political demonstration outside a country's embassy following a mass killing for which the government of that country was being blamed (see paragraph 10). The Court allowed the appeal, replacing a sentence of 18 months' custody with a sentence of 36 weeks suspended for 18 months'.

4.4 Contempt of court

Penalties for contempt of Court are not sentences within the definition of section 222 of the Sentencing Act 2020.

In *Otkritie International Management v Gersamia* [2015] EWHC 821, the Court confirmed the following general principles in relation to penalty for contempt of Court (principles relating to specific forms of contempt have not been included below):

1. The most serious penalty is committal to prison for two years (section 14(1) Contempt of Court Act 1981).

2. Committal may be suspended.

3. Release from a committal to prison will usually be at the half-way point as with other determinate sentences, release will be unconditional and the provisions for licence periods and post-sentence supervision will not apply (section 258 of the Criminal Justice Act 2003). Unfortunately, prisons and probation often miss this point.

4. Committal to prison may serve two distinct purposes: punishment of past contempt and securing compliance.

5. It may be good practice, if the court's sentence includes elements of both, to make clear what period of committal is regarded as appropriate for punishment alone, i.e. what period would be regarded as just if the contemnor were promptly to comply with the order in question.

6. The Court may impose an unlimited fine.

7. Sequestration (seizure of assets) is a possible remedy.

8. Contempt sentences are fact specific.

9. The Court should bear in mind the desirability of keeping offenders, in particular first-time offenders, out of prison.

10. The key questions will be culpability and harm.

11. In all cases, relevant mitigating factors include:

    a. whether, and if so when, the defendant has admitted the contempt;

    b. whether the defendant has expressed remorse;

    c. whether the defendant has, so far as he is able to, complied belatedly with the order or otherwise made amends for the wrong;

    d. the defendant's character and antecedents.

In *R v Jordan* [2024] EWCA Crim 229, the Court of Appeal summarised the principles relating to penalty for contempt in protest cases:

1. The law as to sanctions for contempt is *sui generis* (of its own kind);

2. The custody threshold is not the same as it is in the criminal law generally;

3. The court will take account of the conscientious motives of protestors when they are sentenced;

4. But the quid pro quo for a relatively benign approach to sentence or penalty is a sense of proportion on the part of the offender;

5. The court will have regard to the extent to which a penalty is needed to deter future law breaking, and to further a dialogue

> with the defendant about the need to obey the law and respect the rights of others.

Between September 2021 and November 2021, protestors sat on the M25 in a number of locations. Not long after the protests began, National Highways obtained injunctions prevented people going onto the roadways and slipways. In *National Highways Ltd v Heyatawin & others* [2021] EWHC 3078 (QB), the first set of contempt proceedings arising from these protests, all of the defendants were committed to prison. The sanction was imposed at a point when the protests were ongoing. The Court stated:

> None of the defendants has demonstrated any contrition or understanding of the seriousness of deliberately breaching a court order. Each continues to believe that his or her actions were justified. We have seen nothing to indicate that the defendants will not continue to protest in breach of the M25 Order or other similar orders.
>
> Everything that has been said by or on behalf of the defendants suggests the contrary. In those circumstances, the least sanction we can impose commensurate with the gravity of the defendants' conduct is an order for imprisonment.

In contrast, in *National Highways Limited v Buse & Others* [2021] EWHC 3404 (QB), the second set of contempt proceedings arising from the Insulate Britain protests, the Court took a different approach and found it could suspend some of the committals imposed. By this point the protests had come to an end:

> 52. Further, it is particularly important to note that at the time of the decision in *Heyatawin and others* protests organised by Insulate Britain were continuing over the road network in breach of injunctions granted by the court. In the course of the

> proceedings before us it became clear that there have been no further protests by Insulate Britain or the defendants in breach of the orders made by the court. It is also apparent, if only from the request that Mr Buse be permitted to make an application to purge his contempt this morning, that the "dialogue" referred to in *Cuadrilla*, has begun to take place.
>
> 53. It is also apparent, on the best information available to the claimant, that no further protests are planned at the moment, although the claimant's understanding on intelligence is that further protests might be planned for Spring 2022. In circumstances where it is common ground that the defendants in this case are all conscientious protesters the fact that the protests has stopped is a particularly relevant issue for sanction. This is because a principled aim of the sentencing is to ensure compliance. We have considered whether in these circumstances to suspend the sentences of imprisonment that we will impose. The answer is different for different defendants.

Under the Civil Procedure Rules (CPR81.10) a Defendant against whom a committal order has been made may apply to discharge it. The application should be made by an application notice under Part 23 to the Court that dealt with the committal proceedings. In accordance with CPR81.10(3), the Court dealing with the application 'shall consider all the circumstances and make such order under the law as it thinks fit.'

CHAPTER FIVE

ANCILLARY ORDERS

Criminal Procedure Rules Part 31 deals with behaviour orders including bind overs. CrimPR 31.2 sets out general rules applicable to behaviour orders and bind overs:

> **31.2**—a) The court must not make a behaviour order or impose a bind over unless the person to whom it is directed has had an opportunity—
>
> (a) to consider—
>
> (i) what order is proposed and why, and
>
> (ii) the evidence in support; and
>
> (b) to make representations at a hearing (whether or not that person in fact attends).
>
> (2) That restriction does not apply to making—
>
> (a) an interim behaviour order, but unless other legislation otherwise provides such an order has no effect unless the person to whom it is directed—
>
> (i) is present when it is made; or
>
> (ii) is handed a document recording the order not more than 5 business days after it is made; or

(b) a domestic abuse protection order, but in that event the court must give the defendant an opportunity to make representations—

(i) as soon as is just and convenient, and

(ii) at a hearing of which notice has been given to all parties.

(3) Where the court decides not to make, where it could—

(a) a football banning order; or

(b) a parenting order, after a person under 16 is convicted of an offence,

the court must announce, at a hearing in public, the reasons for its decision.

5.1 Bind over

An individual who is bound over enters into a recognisance: this is an undertaking to pay a sum of money if they fail to comply with the condition of the bind over.

Bind overs have been used as alternatives to proceeding to trial in protest cases as a form of 'preventative justice'. Although they may be proposed by the prosecution and indeed be readily accepted by a defendant who has no intention of engaging in conduct in the future that would put them in breach of the condition, Judges will scrutinise where the criteria for a bind over has really been met.

5.1.1 Procedure

Bind overs can made either on complaint (under section 115 of the Magistrates Court 1980) or of the Court's own motion (under common law and various statutes).

Bind overs on complaint are rare and would require a full hearing of the complaint. Bind overs of the Court's own motion can be made at any point before the conclusion of the criminal proceedings.

CrimPR 31.10 sets out rules in relation to bind overs generally (emphasis added):

> **31.10**—a) Where the court can impose a bind over—
>
> (c) the court must decide, in this sequence—
>
> (i) whether or not to do so and if so in what terms, and then
>
> (ii) the **amount of the recognisance** to require; and
>
> (d) the court may exercise its powers—
>
> (i) **on application or on the court's own initiative**, and
>
> (ii) at a **hearing in public**, as a general rule, or, in exceptional circumstances, in private.
>
> (4) Before imposing a bind over the court must—
>
> (a) take into account, as well as any representations under rule 31.2 (Behaviour orders and bind overs: general rules)—
>
> (i) any evidence introduced, and

(ii) any admission made; and

(b) satisfy itself so that it is sure that the criteria for the bind over are met.

(5) Before deciding the amount of any recognisance to require the court must take into account, as well as any representations under rule 31.2, such information as is readily available about the **financial circumstances of the person to be bound over.**

(6) As a general rule the court **must not impose a bind over for more than 12 months.**

(7) If the court decides to impose a bind over—

(a) **the court must explain, in terms the person to be bound over can understand** (with help if necessary)—

(i) the effect of the court's decision,

(ii) the consequences of refusing to enter into a recognisance,

(iii) the consequences of breaching the bind over, and

(iv) the possibility of appeal; and

(b) the court must announce its decision and reasons at a hearing in public.

(8) A bind over **must be in writing** and must—

(a) describe in ordinary language the conduct from which the person to be bound over must refrain;

(b) specify the amount of the recognisance;

(c) specify the duration of the bind over; and

(d) identify any surety who is not the person to be bound over.

(9) If the Crown Court requires the person to be bound over to come up for judgment, the bind over also must specify—

(a) any date on which, and place and time at which, that person must attend court; or

(b) the means by which that person will be given notice of such a date, place and time.

(10) The court officer must serve the bind over as soon as practicable—

(a) in every case, on the person bound by it; and

(b) as applicable, on each party or other party.

5.1.2 Bind over to keep the peace

In the Magistrates Court and the Crown Court, the court may bind over an individual to keep the peace. A bind over must specify the conduct the individual is to refrain from, it cannot simply require an individual to maintain good behaviour which was held to be too vague (*Hashman & Harrup v UK* [2011] ECHR 1658).

Some key points in relation to bind overs to keep the peace:

1. Bind overs to keep the peace can be made in relation to complainants, witnesses and defendants, including acquitted

defendants and those where prosecution has been unable to proceed.

2. A bind over to keep the peace is not a punishment and will not appear on a criminal record. The power to impose bind overs are exercisable 'not by reason of any offence having been committed, but as a measure of preventive justice' (*Veater v Glennon* [1981] 2 All ER 304).

3. Before imposing a bind over, the Court must be satisfied to the criminal standard that a breach of the peace involving violence, or an imminent threat of violence, has occurred, or that there is a real risk of violence in the future.

4. The length of the order should be proportionate to the harm sought to be avoided (see the Sentencing Guidelines Explanatory Materials on Ancillary Orders).

5. Although the financial circumstances of the individual being bound over must be taken into account, there is no limit on the value of the recognisance.

5.1.3 Bind over to come up for judgment

In the Crown Court, the Court also has the power to bind an individual to come up for judgment. This can be exercised in relation to any offence except where the penalty is fixed by law. This is an alternative to sentence and is a recognisance to come up for judgment and sentence in the event of breach of the condition specified in the bind over. It is most commonly used when an offender from another jurisdiction has committed an offence and expresses they want to return to their own country (see *Crown Court Compendium Part II – Sentencing*).

5.1.4 Refusal to enter into recognisance and breach

A bind over order can only be made with the agreement of the person being bound over. If there is a possibility the person will refuse to enter into a recognisance, the Court should consider alternatives including the continuation of prosecution. If there are no suitable alternatives, the Court may commit the individual into custody although custody should be a last resort (CrimPR 31.11).

In relation to an individual aged between 18 and 20, the court may detain them under section 108 of the Power of Criminal Courts Act 2000. Those under the age of 18 cannot be imprisoned or detained for failure to enter into a recognisance but they can be required to attend an attendance centre (section 60 Power of Criminal Courts Act 2000).

Where an individual breaches a condition stipulated by a bind over, the agreed sum may be forfeit.

Before committing an individual into custody or forfeiting a recognisance, CrimPR 31.11 states that the procedure in CrimPR 48.8 (dealing with contempt of Court) must be followed.

> **48.8**—a) At an enquiry, the court must—
>
> (c) **ensure that the respondent understands** (with help, if necessary) what is alleged, if the enquiry has been postponed from a previous occasion;
>
> (d) explain what the procedure at the enquiry will be; and
>
> (e) **ask whether the respondent admits the conduct in question.**

(11) If the respondent admits the conduct, the court need not receive evidence.

(12) If the respondent does not admit the conduct, the court must consider—

(a) any statement served under rule 48.7;

(b) any other evidence of the conduct;

(c) any evidence introduced by the respondent; and

(d) any representations by the respondent about the conduct.

(13) If the respondent admits the conduct, or the court finds it proved, the court must—

(a) before imposing any punishment for contempt of court, give the respondent an **opportunity to make representations relevant to punishment and a final opportunity to apologise;**

(b) in deciding how to deal with the respondent take into account—

(i) the gravity of the contempt,

(ii) the extent of any admission of the conduct and the stage at which that admission was made,

(iii) any apology and the stage at which that apology was offered, and

(iv) any period during which the respondent was detained pending the enquiry;

(c) **if imprisonment is imposed, impose the shortest period that is commensurate with the preservation of good order in the administration of justice;**

(d) explain, in terms the respondent can understand (with help, if necessary)—

(i) the **reasons for its decision**, including its findings of fact, and

(ii) the **punishment it imposes, and its effect**; and

(e) if a magistrates' court, arrange for the preparation of a **written record** of those findings.

(14) The court that conducts an enquiry—

(a) need not include the same member or members as the court that observed the conduct; but

(b) may do so, unless that would be unfair to the respondent.

The power to impose bind overs are addressed in the Adult Court Bench Book and the Crown Court Bench Book as well as the Sentencing Guidelines Explanatory Materials on Ancillary Orders. The Sentencing Code preserved the existing powers to impose bind overs.

5.2 Criminal behaviour orders

The court may impose a criminal behaviour order (CBO) on adults for a period no less than two years or for an indefinite period (section 334(4)). For offenders under 18, CBOs was be imposed for a period no less than one year and not more than three years (section 334(5)).

The power to impose CBO was introduced by section 22 of the Anti-social Behaviour, Crime and Policing Act 2014 (ABCPA 2014). The statutory provisions are now contained in Chapter 1 of Part 11 of the Sentencing Code.

Statutory Guidance has been issued in relation to the making of CBO.

5.2.1 Test to be applied

A CBO can be made on application on conviction by the prosecution. The Court cannot impose a CBO of its own volition.

The Court may make a CBO against the offender if it (section 331(1):

1. is satisfied to the criminal standard that the offender has engaged in behaviour that caused or was likely to cause harassment, alarm or distress to any person, and
2. considers that making the order will help in preventing the offender from engaging in such behaviour.

The Statutory Guidance confirms an application for a CBO does not require a link between the criminal behaviour which led to the conviction and the anti-social behaviour it addresses for it to be issued by the court.

The Statutory Guidance states:

> *Agencies must make proportionate and reasonable judgements before applying for a CBO, and conditions of an order should not be designed to stop reasonable, trivial or benign behaviour that has not caused, or is unlikely to cause, harassment, alarm or distress to victims or communities.*

In *Khan (Kamran)* [2018] EWCA Crim 1472, [2018] 1 WLR 5419, the Court of Appeal said: 'We do not believe that it was the intention of Parliament that criminal behaviour orders should become a mere matter of box-ticking routine ... such orders are not lightly to be imposed: the court should proceed with a proper degree of caution and circumspection. The Court confirmed that proportionality is intensely fact-specific.

In *Brain* [2020] EWCA Crim 457, [2020] 2 Cr App R (S) 34 (237), the Court of Appeal held that 'the broader historical background' of the offender's behaviour could be taken into account even if it was before the provisions came into effect.

In *DPP v Bulmer* [2015] EWHC 2323 (Admin), [2015] 1 WLR 5159, the Court of Appeal held that the exercise for the court 'remains one of judgment and evaluation' and that Courts 'should proceed with a proper degree of caution and circumspection because such orders are not lightly to be imposed, satisfaction to the criminal standard is not required in what is an evaluative exercise'.

5.2.2 Prohibitions and requirements

Prohibitions and requirements in a criminal behaviour order must, so far as practicable, be such as to avoid (section 331(4))—

a. any interference with the times, if any, at which the offender normally works or attends school or any other educational establishment, and

b. any conflict with the requirements of any other court order to which the offender may be subject.

Where an application relates to an offender under the age of 18, the prosecution must find out the views of the local youth offending team before applying for a criminal behaviour order to be made if the offender will be under the age of 18 when the application is made (section 331(5)).

CBOs may include requirements and prohibitions. The Court may only include requirements and prohibitions that are necessary for the purposes set out above [CASELAW].

The Statutory Guidance indicates that the order may include, for example, attendance at an anger management course where an offender finds it difficult to respond without violence; youth mentoring; a substance misuse awareness session where an offender's anti-social behaviour occurs when they have been drinking or using drugs; or a job readiness course to help an offender get employment and move them away from the circumstances that cause them to commit anti-social behaviour.

An order which includes a requirement must specify a person who is to be responsible for supervising compliance with the requirement (section 333(1)). That person may be a person or an organisation.

Before imposing a requirement the court must receive evidence from the person or organisation that would be responsible for supervising the requirement.

If considering multiple requirements, the court must consider the compatibility of the requirements with each other (section 333(3)).

The person or organisation supervising any requirements must do the following (section 333(4)):

1. to make any necessary arrangements in connection with the requirements for which the person has responsibility (the "relevant requirements");

2. to promote the offender's compliance with the relevant requirements;

3. if the person considers that the offender has complied with all of the relevant requirements, or has failed to comply with a relevant requirement, inform the appropriate chief officer of police.

The court may specify periods for which particular requirements or prohibitions have effect (section 333(6)).

In *R (Cooke) v DPP* [2008] EWHC 2703 (Admin), (2008) 172 JP 596 the Court held that where the offender is *capable* of understanding the terms of a CBO but *incapable* of complying with them, 'so that the only effect of the order will be to criminalise behaviour over which he has no control', that 'will indicate that the order will not be helpful and will not satisfy the second condition' (at 24]).

In *Boness* [2005] EWCA Crim 2395, [2006] 1 Cr App R (S) 120 (690) the Court held that prohibitions or requirements must be 'reasonable, proportionate, realistic, practical, clear and enforceable'.

In *P (Shane Tony)* [2004] EWCA Crim 287, [2004] 2 Cr App R (S) 63 (343) the Court held that 'the terms of the order must be precise and capable of being understood by offender'.

5.2.3 Offences

The offender may commit an offence if they fail without reasonable to do something required by the order or without reasonable excuse does something they are prohibited from doing (section 339(1)) by a CBO.

Breaching a CBO is punishable by the maximum of five years imprisonment (section 339(2)). A conditional discharge is not available for breach of a conditional discharge (section 339(3)).

In relation to proceedings for breach of a CBO relating to offenders under 18, automatic reporting restrictions under section 49 of the Children and Young Persons Act 1933 but the court has the power to prohibit publication of certain matters under section 45 of the Youth Justice and Criminal Evidence Act 1999. If the court does not exercise its discretion to impose reporting restrictions under section 45, it must give its reasons for doing so.

5.2.4 Review for offenders under 18

Where an offender is under 18 years old, a CBO must be subject to an annual review (section 337) to be carried out by the chief officer of police of the police force maintained for the police area in which the offender resides or appears to be residing.

A review must include consideration of:

a. the extent to which the offender has complied with the order;

b. the adequacy of any support available to the offender to help the offender comply with it;

c. any matters relevant to the question whether an application should be made for the order to be varied or discharged.

5.2.5 Variation or discharge

An application may be made for the variation or discharge of a CBO (section 336). An application is made to the Court that originally imposed the order.

An application can be made by the following:

1. The offender
2. The prosecution

If varying a CBO, the court may vary the order:

a. to include an additional prohibition or requirement in the order, or

b. to extend the period for which a prohibition or requirement has effect.

5.2.6 Appeal

On appeal against the making of a CBO by the Magistrates Court is to the Crown Court by way of right. An appeal against the making of a CBO by the Crown Court is by way of permission to the Court of Appeal.

Challenge to the refusal to make a CBO would be by way of case stated or judicial review.

5.2.7 Legal Aid

Pursuant to section 14(b) of the Legal Aid, Sentencing and Punishment of Offenders Act 2012, proceedings relating to CBO are covered by the representation order covering the original offence or offences.

5.3 Football banning orders

The Football Spectators Act 1989 contains powers to exclude individuals from attendance at football matches.

The Court **must** make a football banning order where an offender has been convicted of a relevant offence, unless the court considers that there are particular circumstances relating to the offence or to the offender which would make it unjust in all the circumstances to do so. Where a football banning order is not made the Court must state in open Court the reasons for not going so (CrimPR 31.2 (3)(a)).

It is worth noting that the test was amended by the Police, Crime, Sentencing and Courts Act 2022. Prior to amendment, the Court had to be satisfied that there are reasonable grounds to believe that making a banning order would help to prevent violence or disorder at or in connection with any regulated football matches, it must make such an order in respect of the offender.

In *R v Boggild* [2011] EWCA Crim 1928, the Court held that it is "palpably not the scheme of the Act to make a football banning order the inevitable consequence of a football related conviction" (para 20).

In *R v Hughes* [2005] EWCA Crim 2537, followed by *R (White) v Blackfriars Crown Court* [2008] EWHC 510 (Admin) and cited in *Boggild*, the Court held that deterrence of football banning hooligans generally is a legitimate factor in the decision to make a FBO. In *Boggild* the Court warned that it does not follow that general deterrence, although a legitimate factor, is the determinative factor.

Most of the caselaw dealing with FBO including *Boggild* pre-dates this amendment so caution is required to ensure the correct test is addressed.

The court may impose a football banning order (FBO) for a period no less than three years and for no more than five years unless sentenced immediate imprisonment where the period is no less than six years and no more than 10 years.

5.3.1 Test to be applied

A FBO can be made on conviction or on complaint (by the relevant chief officer or the DPP). In the context of protest, an application for a FBO on complaint will rarely arise so is not addresses in detail in this chapter.

The following test is to be applied where an application is made on complaint:

1. The Respondent has at any time caused or contributed to any violence or disorder in the United Kingdom or elsewhere (section 14B(2)).

2. The court is satisfied that there are reasonable grounds to believe that making a banning order would help to prevent violence or disorder at or in connection with any regulated football matches (section 14B(4)(b)).

Where an offender is convicted of a relevant offence, the Court **must** make a FBO unless the court considers that there are particular circumstances relating to the offence or to the offender which would make it unjust in all the circumstances to do so (section 14A(2)).

FBO have been made following conviction where protestors have been involved in pitch incursions.

5.3.2 Procedure

Orders on complaint

Where an application is made on complaint, the Magistrates Court may when adjourning proceedings may remand the Respondent. If remanding on bail, the Court may impose conditions of bail including not to leave (a) not to leave England and Wales before his appearance before the court, and (b) if the control period relates to a regulated football match outside the United Kingdom or to an external tournament which includes such matches, to surrender his passport to a police constable, if he has not already done so (section 14B(6)).

Orders on conviction

The Court may consider evidence led by the prosecution or the defence (section 14A(3A)). It is immaterial whether evidence led would have been admissible in the proceedings in which the offender was convicted (section 14A(3B)).

The relevant offences are set out in schedule 1 to the Football Spectators Act 1989 and include public order and violent offences (but only if they were committed at or in connection with a football match, or when travelling to or from a football match), as well as specific football offences.

Under paragraphs (g) to (o), the offence will only be a relevant offence if the Court makes a declaration that it was related to a football match. The legislation offers no definition of when this declaration will be made. In *R v Doyle* [2012] EWCA Crim 995 the Court held that it was not enough that the offence would not have occurred 'but for' the fact that the offender was on their way to or from a match.

Pitch incursions will generally be charged under section 4 of the Football (Offences) Act 1991 as well as aggravated trespass and so would generally attract football banning orders.

A FBO on conviction can only be made in addition to sentence or an offender being conditionally discharged.

Where a declaration of relevance is required, the prosecution must serve notice at least five days before the start of trial that it proposes to show that it was an offence related to a football match or organisation (section 23(1)).

The Court may still go on to make a declaration of relevance even where the requisite notice has not been given if the offender waives the requirement to give notice or the Court is satisfied the interests of justice do not require more notice to be given (section 23(2)).

5.3.3 Prohibitions and requirements

A FBO **must** include the following prohibition:

1. Prohibition from entering any premises for the purpose of attending a regulated football match in England and Wales (section 14(4)(a)).

A FBO **must** include the following requirements:

2. Reporting to a specified police station within 5 days of the order being imposed (section 14E(2)).

3. Notification of the following within 7 days (section 14E(2A) and (2B)):

    a. Change of name

    b. Change of address

    c. Acquisition of a temporary address

    d. Loss of passport

    e. Receipt of a new passport

    f. An appeal made in relation to the order

    g. An application made under section 14H(2) for termination of the order

    h. An appeal made under section 23(3) against the making of a declaration of relevance in respect of an offence of which he has been convicted.

4. Surrender of passport in advance of regulated football matches outside the United Kingdom (Section 14E(3))

The Court may also impose additional requirements as it sees fit (section 14G(1)).

A 'regulated football match' means 'an association football match (whether in the UK or elsewhere) which is a prescribed match or a match of a prescribed description' (section 14(2)).

Section 22A(1) allows for the Secretary of State to prescribe matches. The Football Spectators (Prescription Order) 2022 (SI 2022 No. 617) describes the football matches both within and outside England and Wales which are regulated football matches.

5.3.4 Offences

Failure to comply with any requirement of a FBO is an offence punishable by six months imprisonment or a level 5 fine (section 14J).

There is no power within the legislation for a FBO to be extended upon conviction for breach.

5.3.5 Variation or discharge

The offender or the person who applied for the FBO may apply to the Court that made it to impose, replace or omit additional (discretionary) requirements (section 14G(2)).

After at least two-thirds of the FBO is complete, the offender may apply to the Court which imposed it to terminate it (section 14H(1)). On such an application the Court must have regard to the offender's character, his conduct since the banning order was made, the nature of the offence or conduct which led to it and any other circumstances which appear to it to be relevant (section 14H(3)).

If an application to terminate a FBO is refused, no further application may be made within six months (section 14H(4)).

The Court may order the applicant to pay all or any part of the costs of an application (section 14H(5)).

5.3.6 Appeal

Appeal against the making of a FBO is as an appeal against sentence. The prosecution may appeal against the refusal to impose a FBO under section 14A(5A).

Appeal against the making of a declaration of relevance is as if it were an appeal against sentence. If the declaration of relevance is reversed on appeal, a banning order made following the declaration will be quashed (section 23(3) and (4)).

5.3.7 Legal Aid

Pursuant to section 14(b) of the Legal Aid, Sentencing and Punishment of Offenders Act 2012, proceedings relating to FBO are covered by criminal Legal Aid.

Legal Aid to defend an application for a FBO on complaint is covered by a representation order. For applications on conviction, the representation order covering the original offence will cover proceedings.

5.4 Serious disruption prevention orders

Part 2 of the Public Order 2023 introduced the power to imposed serious disruption prevention orders (SDPO). These are orders which can be imposed on offenders aged 18 or over for a period between one week and two years.

SDPO can be made on application by the prosecution on conviction for a protest-related offence or on application by a chief officer of police or a chief constable of the British Transport Police, Civil Nuclear Constabulary or Ministry of Defence Police.

Statutory Guidance has been issued in relation to the making of SDPO.

Caselaw relevant to other restrictive orders, such as the caselaw outlined above on criminal behaviour orders, will be relevant to applications for SDPO.

5.4.1 Test to be applied

A SDPO can be made on application by the prosecution or the police. The Court cannot impose a SDPO of its own volition.

The following test is to be applied when considering an application for a SDPO **on conviction:**

1. The Court must be satisfied on the balance of probabilities that the offence the offender has been **convicted of is a protest-related offence** (section 20(2)(a)). A protest-related offence is defined as an offence which is directly related to a protest (section 32).

2. The court must be satisfied on the balance of probabilities that within the last 5 years after section 20 has come into force, the offender has, in relation to a **different protest or on a different day**, either:

    a. committed **another protest-related offence** for which the individual was convicted, or

    b. committed a **protest-related breach of an injunction** for which the individual was found in contempt of court.

The following test is to be applied when considering an application for a SDPO **on application:**

1. The court must be satisfied on the balance of probabilities that the offender has **on at least two occasions** in the previous five years (but only after the offender turned 16 and after section 21 came into force)

    a. committed a **protest-related offence** for which P was convicted, or

    b. committed a **protest-related breach** of an injunction for which P was found in contempt of court,

2. The offender's conduct in relation to each occasion

    a. related to a different protest, or

    b. took place on a different day, and

    c. has not been taken into account when making any previous serious disruption prevention order in respect of the offender

Whether an order is made on conviction or on application, the court must be satisfied that it is necessary to make the order for the purpose of:

a. Preventing the offender from:

    i. committing a protest-related offence or a protest-related breach of an injunction,

    ii. carrying out activities related to a protest that result in, or are likely to result in, serious disruption to two or more individuals or to an organisation, in England and Wales, or

iii. causing or contributing to the commission by any other individual of a protest-related offence or a protest-related breach of an injunction, or the carrying out by any other individual of activities related to a protest that result in, or are likely to result in, serious disruption to two or more individuals, or to an organisation, in England and Wales.

b. Protecting two or more individuals, or an organisation, in England and Wales from the risk of serious disruption arising from:

iv. a protest-related offence,

v. a protest-related breach of an injunction, or

vi. activities related to a protest.

The court must not take into account any conduct that has been taken into account for the purposes of a previous SDPO imposed on the individual nor any conduct which took place when the individual was aged 15 or under (section 20(4)(b)). The court must also not take into account any conduct which occurred before the commencement of section 20 of the Public Order Act 2023.

Given the applicable tests, it is essential to understand the timeline and details of any previous offences and convictions. It is increasingly common for individuals to be prosecuted and subject to contempt proceedings for the same offence.

Careful consideration should be given to whether or not to accept an offence or breach of injunction is protest-related.

5.4.2 Serious disruption

The cases in which individuals or an organisation may suffer serious disruption **include**, in particular, where the individuals or the organisation (section 34(1)):

a. Are by way of physical obstruction prevented, or hindered to more than a minor degree, from carrying out

   i. their day-to-day activities (including in particular the making of a journey),

   ii. construction or maintenance works, or

   iii. activities related to such works,

b. are prevented from making or receiving, or suffer a delay that is more than minor to the making or receiving of, a delivery of a time-sensitive product, or

c. are prevented from accessing, or suffer a disruption that is more than minor to the accessing of, any essential goods or any essential service.

The definition above of serious disruption is not exhaustive as highlighted in the Statutory Guidance.

The definition of '**time-sensitive product**' means a product whose value or use to its consumers may be significantly reduced by a delay in the supply of the product to them (section 34(2)(a)).

Accessing **essential goods or essential services** includes in particular a reference to accessing (section 34(2)(b):

1. the supply of money, food, water, energy or fuel,
2. a system of communication,
3. a place of worship,
4. a transport facility,
5. an educational institution, or
6. a service relating to health.

5.4.3 Procedure

The court may only make a SDPO if in addition to a sentence or conditional discharge (not an absolute discharge).

The court may adjourn an application for a SDPO even after the offender has been sentenced. If the offender does not appear, the court may (section 20(11)):

1. further adjourn the proceedings,
2. issue a warrant for P's arrest, or
3. hear the proceedings in P's absence.

The court may not issue a warrant unless it is satisfied that the offender has been given adequate notice of the time and place of the adjourned proceedings (section 20(11)).

The court may consider evidence led by the prosecution or the offender (section (2)(8)). It does not matter whether the evidence would have been admissible in the proceedings for the current offence (section 20(9)).

5.4.4 Prohibitions and requirements

SDPOs must include notification requirements and may include requirements and prohibitions. The Court may only include requirements and prohibitions that are necessary for the purposes set out above.

Requirements may have the effect of requiring the offender (a) to present themselves to a particular person at a particular place at, or between, particular times on particular days (b) to remain at a particular place for particular periods (section 22(2)).

Prohibitions may have the effect of requiring the offender from doing the following (section 22(4)):

a. being in or entering a particular place or area;

b. being in or entering a particular place or area between particular times on particular days;

c. being in or entering a particular place or area between particular times on any day;

d. being with particular persons;

e. participating in particular activities;

f. having particular articles with them;

g. using the internet to facilitate or encourage persons to—

   i. commit a protest-related offence or a protest-related breach of an injunction, or

   ii. carry out activities related to a protest that result in, or are likely to result in, serious disruption to two or more individuals, or to an organisation, in England and Wales.

The Statutory Guidance indicates that the order may include, for example, prohibiting an individual from attending protests organised by a group which the individual's past conduct is associated with, for the duration of the order, or requiring an individual to attend a police station each day during a week of planned protest activity by that group.

The requirements or prohibitions which are imposed on a person by a serious disruption prevention order must, so far as practicable, be such as to avoid:

a. any conflict with the person's religious beliefs, and

b. any interference with the times, if any, at which the person normally works or attends any educational establishment (section 22(8)).

An order which includes a requirement other than notification requirements must specify a person who is to be responsible for supervising compliance with the requirement (section 23(1)). That person may be a person or an organisation (section 23(2)).

Before imposing a requirement the court must receive evidence from the person or organisation that would be responsible for supervising the requirement (section 23(3)).

If considering multiple requirements, the court must consider the compatibility of the requirements with each other (section 23(4)).

The person or organisation supervising any requirements must do the following (section 23(5) and (7)):

4. to make any necessary arrangements in connection with the requirements for which the person has responsibility (the "relevant requirements");

5. to promote P's compliance with the relevant requirements;

6. if the person considers that the offender has complied with all of the relevant requirements, or has failed to comply with a relevant requirement, inform the appropriate chief officer of police.

Where an offender is in custody or on licence, the court may order that it does not take effect until the offender is no longer in custody or on licence (section 25(3)). The court may specify periods for which particular requirements or prohibitions have effect (section 25(5)). Where a court makes a serious disruption prevention order in respect of a person and the person is already subject to such an order, the earlier order ceases to have effect (section 25(6)).

An order must specify the reasons for making the order and penalties that may be imposed for breaching the order (section 26). On making a serious disruption prevention order the court must in ordinary language explain to offender the effects of the order.

5.4.5 Notification requirements

A SDPO must imposed notification requirements (section 24(1)). The offender must notify the police within three days of the order being imposed of the following (section 24(2) and (3)):

1. The offender's name on the day that the notification is given and any other names used,
2. The offender's home address on that day, and
3. The address of any other premises at which, on that day, the offender regularly resides or stays.

The offender must notify within three days any of the following changes (section 24(4) and (5)):

1. Using a name that has not previously been notified
2. Change of home address
3. Deciding to live for a period of one month or more at any premises not previously notified

'Home address' is defined as the offender's main or sole resident or if there is none, the place where they can usually be found (section 32).

Notification requirements can be satisfied by attending a police station local to where the offender lives and communicating the information orally to an authorised officer (section 24(6)).

5.4.6 Offences

The offender may commit an offence if they fail without reasonable to do something required by the order or without reasonable excuse does something they are prohibited from doing by a SDPO or notifies information which they know to be false (section 27(1)).

Breaching a SDPO is punishable by the maximum for summary offences (six month imprisonment at the time of writing) (section 27(2) and (3)). For offenders under 18 the maximum is two years detention and training order (DTO).

5.4.7 Variation, renewal or discharge

An application may be made for the variation renewal or discharge of a SDPO (section 28). An application is made to the Court that originally imposed the order.

An application can be made by the following:

5. The offender
6. The chief officer of police for the police area in which the offender lives;
7. A chief officer of police who believes that offender is in, or is intending to come to, the chief officer's police area;
8. If the application for the order was made by a chief officer of police other than one within paragraph (b) or (c), the chief officer by whom the application was made;

9. The chief officer of police for a police area in which the offender committed an offence on the basis of which the order was made;

10. Where the order was made following an application by a constable as specified in subsection (3), that constable.

The court must hear from the person making the order and any other person who wishes to be heard (section 28(5)).

The court may only vary or renew a SDPO if it considers that to do so is necessary for one of the statutory purposes of SDPO as outlined previously. **The court may only renew a SDPO once.** If varying or renewing a SDPO, the court may:

c. vary a serious disruption prevention order so as to

    i. extend the period for which the order has effect,

    ii. extend the period for which a requirement or prohibition imposed by the order has effect, or

    iii. impose an additional prohibition or requirement on P, or

d. renew a serious disruption prevention order

5.4.8 Appeal

Section 29 sets out the provisions in relation to appeals relating to SDPO. An appeal against the making of a SDPO is as follows:

1. Appeal against an order on conviction, as if the order were a sentence passed on the offender

2. Appeal against an order on complaint, to the Crown Court

3. Appeal against a refusal to make an order, is as if it were an appeal against sentence

4. Appeal against decisions in relation to variation, from the Magistrates Court to the Crown Court and from the Crown Court to the Court of Appeal

5.4.9 Legal Aid

Pursuant to section 14(b) of the Legal Aid, Sentencing and Punishment of Offenders Act 2012, SDPO made on conviction are covered by the representation order covering the original offence or offences.

The Criminal Legal Aid (General) (Amendment) Regulations 2024 extended Legal Aid to cover stand-alone applications, variation, renewal, extension and discharge of Serious Disruption Prevention Orders ("SDPOs"), and appeals related to those proceedings. A represented order is applied for on the Apply for Criminal Legal Aid service.

5.5 Restraining orders

5.5.1 Restraining order on conviction

The provisions for imposing restraining orders are now contained within section 359 and 360 of the Sentencing Code.

A restraining order is an order prohibiting a person from doing specified things, usually from making contact with a specified person or attending a specified address, for the purposes of protecting victims of offending from future harassment or conduct causing fear of violence (section 360). Conduct includes speech and harassment includes alarming or causing distress (section 364).

An order may be made for the protection of an individual or a group individuals "provided those groups are sufficiently clearly defined for them to know who they are and for the person against whom the order is made to know who they are, so that everybody will be clear what persons are included in the order and what persons are not" (*R v Buxton* [2010] EWCA Crim 1339).

The terms of the order should be proportionate to the harm that it is sought to prevent (*R v Khellaf* [2016] EWCA Crim 1297).

A restraining order may be imposed for a specified period or until further order (section 359).

5.5.2 Restraining order on acquittal

A Court has the power under section 5A(1) of the Protection from Harassment Act 1997 to make a restraining order on acquittal if it considers it necessary to do so to protect a person (or persons) from harassment by the defendant.

An order may be imposed for a specified period or until further order.

There must be evidence which shows a risk of harassment in the future. Where the application is sought after a full trial, the evidence maybe clear. A number of appeals against the making of an order on acquittal have been allowed where there was insufficient evidence to justify the making of an order (see *R v Baldwin* [2021] EWCA Crim 703 and *R v Khan* [2021] EWCA Crim 1526).

Restraining orders are civil and civil rules of evidence will apply.

There is a danger that restraining orders on acquittal are treated as alternatives to prosecution where the prosecution case is lacking. They should not be agreed to without careful consideration and the Court should refuse to impose an order where the prosecution have failed to adduce any evidence upon which to make the application.

5.5.3 Offences

It is an offence punishable by a maximum of five years imprisonment to breach a restraining order without reasonable excuse (section 360 of the Sentencing Code and section 5A of the Protection from Harassment Act 1997).

5.5.4 Variation or discharge

The prosecutor, defendant or any person named in the order may apply to the Court for the order to be varied or discharged (section 361 of the Sentencing Code and section 5(4) of the Protection from Harassment Act 1997).

Although the legislation does not include any express requirement to satisfy the Court that there has been a material change in circumstances, an application to discharge an order should not be used as an appeal against original making of the order. Although the Court in *R v Jackson* [2021] EWCA Crim 901 did not consider there to be a "hard-edged requirement to prove a change of circumstances since the order was first made" the Court went onto say "we would anticipate that most successful applications to extend or tighten a restraining order will be based on material which was not before the sentencing court and which justifies a change of approach" (para 35).

5.5.5 Appeal

On appeal against the making of a restraining order by the Magistrates Court is to the Crown Court by way of right. An appeal against the making of a restraining order by the Crown Court is by way of permission to the Court of Appeal.

5.5.6 Legal Aid

Pursuant to section 14(b) of the Legal Aid, Sentencing and Punishment of Offenders Act 2012, applications for restraining orders on conviction are covered by the representation order covering the original offence or offences.

Proceedings relating to restraining orders on acquittal are prescribed proceedings and covered by criminal legal aid. An application for a representation order will need to be made through the Apply for Criminal Legal Aid service.

5.6 Rehabilitation of Offenders Act 1974

Rehabilitation periods refer to the period after which a conviction is considered 'spent'. Generally the provisions in relation to rehabilitation periods will depend on the sentence passed. As set out in section 5(2) of the Rehabilitation of Offenders Act 1974, where a relevant order is imposed, the rehabilitation period will end on the last day the order is to take effect.

Relevant orders are set out at section 5(8) and include a bind over and any order which imposes a disqualification, disability, prohibition, penalty, requirement or restriction, or is otherwise intended to regulate the behaviour of the person convicted.

Defendants should be advised of the impact of rehabilitation periods. Even where orders may not seem too onerous, they can have a significant impact on professional and personal lives.

The Ministry of Justice has published Guidance on the Rehabilitation of Offenders Act 1974 and The Exceptions Order 1975.

CHAPTER SIX

PRACTICAL APPROACH

There has without doubt been a shift in sentencing in protest cases with unprecedent prison sentences being imposed. Where once more lenient sentencing was expected in the context of protest, Courts appear to be treating organised disruptive protest as particularly serious.

As the Court is not required to give any particular reduction for conscientious motive or declare what reduction has been given, there is a risk that Judge will just pay lip-service to conscientious motive.

To avoid the sentencing inflation warned of by the Court of Appeal in *R v Hallam* [2025] EWCA Crim 199, it is important to properly engage in the general sentencing principles before turning to conscientious motives.

It goes without saying that the protest caselaw cited in this book would not exist without the real people whose cases they relate to, people who have acted for conscientious motives to bring about change in the world. There is a risk that protestors can be simply viewed as a collective, overlooking their individual circumstances and the individual considerations relevant to sentencing.

There may be many reasons to justify lower sentences based on the circumstances of the Defendant or the case, whether it be health, age, dependants or profession. These will need to be fully explored and evidenced.

Many protestors will have been subject to injunctions or entered into undertakings mirroring the terms of an injunction. Where injunctions have been dealt with in the High Court judgments will be published and can be used as evidence in support of mitigation.

APPENDIX A

COMMON OFFENCES

The table below sets out common offences that arise in protest cases.

Offence	Legislation	Maximum Sentence	Guidelines
Breach of a section 12 condition on a procession – participant	Section 12(5) and (9) Public Order Act 1986	Level 4 fine	No offence specific guidelines. Consider the General Guidelines.
Breach of a section 12 condition on a procession – organiser	Section 12(4) and (8) of the Public Order Act 1986	Maximum for summary offences – six months imprisonment at the time of writing	No offence specific guidelines. Consider the General Guidelines.
Breach of a section 14 condition on an assembly – participant	Section 14(5) and (9) Public Order Act 1986	Level 4 fine	No offence specific guidelines. Consider the General Guidelines.

Breach of a section 14 condition on a procession – organiser	Section 14(4) and (8) of the Public Order Act 1986	Maximum for summary offences – six months imprisonment at the time of writing	No offence specific guidelines. Consider the General Guidelines.
Aggravated trespass	Section 68 of the Criminal Justice and Public Order Act 1994	Three months imprisonment	No offence specific guidelines. Consider the General Guidelines.
Failure to comply with a direction to leave land	Section 69 of the Criminal Justice and Public Order Act 1994	Three months imprisonment	No offence specific guidelines. Consider the General Guidelines.
Obstructing the highway	Section 137 of the Highways Act 1980	Six months imprisonment	No offence specific guidelines. Consider the General Guidelines.

Locking-on	Section 1 of the Public Order Act 2023	The maximum term for summary offences (six months imprisonment at the time of writing)	No offence specific guidelines. Consider the General Guidelines.
Going equipped for locking-on	Section 2 of the Public Order Act 2023	Fine only	No offence specific guidelines. Consider the General Guidelines.
Causing serious disruption by tunnelling	Section 3 of the Public Order Act 2023	Three years	No offence specific guidelines. Consider the General Guidelines and relevant caselaw (*R v Hallam*).
Causing serious disruption by being present in a tunnel	Section 4 of the Public Order Act 2023	Three years	No offence specific guidelines. Consider the General Guidelines and relevant caselaw (*R v Hallam*).

Being equipped for tunnelling	Section 5 of the Public Order Act 2023	The maximum term for summary offences (six months imprisonment at the time of writing)	No offence specific guidelines. Consider the General.
Interference with national infrastructure	Section 7 of the Public Order 2023	12 months imprisonment	No offence specific guidelines. Consider the General Guidelines.
Public nuisance	Section 78 of the Police, Crime, Sentencing and Courts Act 2022	10 years imprisonment	No offence specific guidelines. Consider the General Guidelines and relevant caselaw (*R v Trowland* and *R v Hallam*).

Criminal damage (other than by fire)	Section 1 and 4 of the Criminal Damage Act 1971	Criminal damage under £5000 (other than a memorial) – three months imprisonment Criminal damage exceeding £5000 or criminal damage to memorials – 10 years imprisonment	Offence specific guidelines available covering an offence range from discharge to 4 years imprisonment. See also *R v Hallam*.

MORE BOOKS BY
LAW BRIEF PUBLISHING

A selection of our other titles available now:-

'A Practical Guide to Probation Breaches and Other Applications' by Mark Thomas
'A Practical Guide to Remarriage and Divorce' by Cordelia Williams & Claire Howard
'A Practical Guide to Privacy, Transparency, Reporting Restrictions and Closed Proceedings in the Court of Protection' by Laura Mannering
'Beaumont on Barristers – A Guide to Defending Disciplinary Proceedings (Second Edition)' by Marc Beaumont
'A Practical Guide to Payments for Environmental Services' by Ben Sharples
'A Practical Guide to the Law of Pregnancy and Maternity at Work' by Rebecca Thomas
'A Practical Guide to Redundancy – Second Edition' by Philip Hyland & Collette Moore
'A Practical Guide to International Issues for Scottish Family Lawyers' by Susie Mountain, Donna McKay, Ken MacDonald
'A Practical Guide to the Law on Deprivation of Liberty' by Ben Troke
'A Practical Guide to Rights over Airspace and Subsoil – Second Edition' by Daniel Gatty
'A Practical Guide to the Law in Relation to Inquests' by Ramya Nagesh
'A Practical Guide to the Construction and Rectification of Wills and Trust Instruments (Second Edition)' by Edward Hewitt
'A Practical Guide to Data Protection in Social Housing' by Clare Paterson
'A Practical Guide to Spousal Maintenance – Second Edition' by Liz Cowell
'A Practical Guide to International Parental Child Abduction Law (England and Wales)' by Dr Onyója Momoh
'A Practical Guide to Deprivation of British Citizenship' by Sean Ell
'A Practical Guide to Commercial Property Service Charges' by Rachel Garton
'A Practical Guide to Clinical Negligence – Third Edition' by Geoffrey Simpson-Scott (Geoff)
'A Practical Guide to the Rights of Grandparents in Children Proceedings – Second Edition' by Stuart Barlow

'The Electronic Communications Code: A Practical Guide – Second Edition' by Kerry Bretherton KC, James Castle, Mark Loveday
'A Practical Guide to the Independent School Standards – September 2023 Edition' by Sarah McKimm
'A Practical Guide to Estate Administration and Crypto Assets' by Richard Marshall
'A Practical Guide to Parental Alienation in Private and Public Law Children Cases' by Sam King QC & Frankie Shama
'Contested Heritage – Removing Art from Land and Historic Buildings' by Richard Harwood QC, Catherine Dobson, David Sawtell
'The Limits of Separate Legal Personality: When Those Running a Company Can Be Held Personally Liable for Losses Caused to Third Parties Outside of the Company' by Dr Mike Wilkinson
'A Practical Guide to Transgender Law' by Robin Moira White & Nicola Newbegin
'A Practical Guide to 'Stranded Spouses' in Family Law' by Mani Singh Basi
'A Practical Guide to Residential Freehold Conveyancing' by Lorraine Richardson
'A Practical Guide to Pensions on Divorce for Lawyers' by Bryan Scant
'A Practical Guide to Challenging Sham Marriage Allegations in Immigration Law' by Priya Solanki
'A Practical Guide to Digital Communications Evidence in Criminal Law' by Sam Willis
'A Practical Guide to Legal Rights in Scotland' by Sarah-Jane Macdonald
'A Practical Guide to New Build Conveyancing' by Paul Sams & Rebecca East
'A Practical Guide to Inherited Wealth on Divorce' by Hayley Trim
'A Practical Guide to Practice Direction 12J and Domestic Abuse in Private Law Children Proceedings' by Rebecca Cross & Malvika Jaganmohan
'A Practical Guide to Confiscation and Restraint' by Narita Bahra QC, John Carl Townsend, David Winch
'A Practical Guide to the Law of Forests in Scotland' by Philip Buchan
'A Practical Guide to Health and Medical Cases in Immigration Law' by Rebecca Chapman & Miranda Butler
'A Practical Guide to Bad Character Evidence for Criminal Practitioners by Aparna Rao
'A Practical Guide to Extradition Law post-Brexit' by Myles Grandison et al
'A Practical Guide to Hoarding and Mental Health for Housing Lawyers' by Rachel Coyle

‘Stephens on Contractual Indemnities’ by Richard Stephens
‘A Practical Guide to the EU Succession Regulation’ by Richard Frimston
‘A Practical Guide to Solicitor and Client Costs – Second Edition’ by Robin Dunne
‘Constructive Dismissal – Practice Pointers and Principles’ by Benjimin Burgher
‘A Practical Guide to Religion and Belief Discrimination Claims in the Workplace’ by Kashif Ali
‘A Practical Guide to the Law of Medical Treatment Decisions’ by Ben Troke
‘Fundamental Dishonesty and QOCS in Personal Injury Proceedings: Law and Practice’ by Jake Rowley
‘A Practical Guide to the Law in Relation to School Exclusions’ by Charlotte Hadfield & Alice de Coverley
‘A Practical Guide to Divorce for the Silver Separators’ by Karin Walker
‘The Right to be Forgotten – The Law and Practical Issues’ by Melissa Stock
‘A Practical Guide to Planning Law and Rights of Way in National Parks, the Broads and AONBs’ by James Maurici QC, James Neill et al
‘A Practical Guide to Election Law’ by Tom Tabori
‘A Practical Guide to the Law in Relation to Surrogacy’ by Andrew Powell
‘A Practical Guide to Claims Arising from Fatal Accidents – Second Edition’ by James Patience
‘A Practical Guide to Asbestos Claims’ by Jonathan Owen & Gareth McAloon
‘A Practical Guide to Stamp Duty Land Tax in England and Northern Ireland’ by Suzanne O’Hara
‘A Practical Guide to the Law of Farming Partnerships’ by Philip Whitcomb
‘A Practical Guide to the Law of Unlawful Eviction and Harassment – Second Edition’ by Stephanie Lovegrove
‘A Practical Guide to Costs in Personal Injury Claims – Second Edition’ by Matthew Hoe
‘A Practical Guide to the General Data Protection Regulation (GDPR) – Second Edition’ by Keith Markham
‘A Practical Guide to Working with Litigants in Person and McKenzie Friends in Family Cases’ by Stuart Barlow
‘Protecting Unregistered Brands: A Practical Guide to the Law of Passing Off’ by Lorna Brazell
‘A Practical Guide to Secondary Liability and Joint Enterprise Post-Jogee’ by Joanne Cecil & James Mehigan

'A Practical Guide to the Pre-Action RTA Claims Protocol for Personal Injury Lawyers' by Antonia Ford
'A Practical Guide to Neighbour Disputes and the Law' by Alexander Walsh
'A Practical Guide to Coercive Control for Legal Practitioners and Victims' by Rachel Horman
'A Practical Guide to the Law of Driverless Cars – Second Edition'
by Alex Glassbrook, Emma Northey & Scarlett Milligan
'A Practical Guide to TOLATA Claims' by Greg Williams
'A Practical Guide to Elderly Law – Second Edition' by Justin Patten
'A Practical Guide to Responding to Housing Disrepair and Unfitness Claims' by Iain Wightwick
'A Practical Guide to the Law of Bullying and Harassment in the Workplace' by Philip Hyland
'How to Be a Freelance Solicitor: A Practical Guide to the SRA-Regulated Freelance Solicitor Model' by Paul Bennett
'A Practical Guide to Prison Injury Claims' by Malcolm Johnson
'A Practical Guide to Advising Clients at the Police Station' by Colin Stephen McKeown-Beaumont
'A Practical Guide to Antisocial Behaviour Injunctions – Second Edition' by Iain Wightwick
'Practical Mediation: A Guide for Mediators, Advocates, Advisers, Lawyers, and Students in Civil, Commercial, Business, Property, Workplace, and Employment Cases' by Jonathan Dingle with John Sephton
'The Mini-Pupillage Workbook' by David Boyle
'A Practical Guide to Crofting Law' by Brian Inkster
'A Practical Guide to the Law of Domain Names and Cybersquatting' by Andrew Clemson
'A Practical Guide to the Law of Gender Pay Gap Reporting' by Harini Iyengar
'NHS Whistleblowing and the Law' by Joseph England
'Employment Law and the Gig Economy' by Nigel Mackay & Annie Powell
'A Practical Guide to Noise Induced Hearing Loss (NIHL) Claims' by Andrew Mckie, Ian Skeate, Gareth McAloon
'An Introduction to Beauty Negligence Claims – A Practical Guide for the Personal Injury Practitioner' by Greg Almond
'Intercompany Agreements for Transfer Pricing Compliance' by Paul Sutton
'Zen and the Art of Mediation' by Martin Plowman
'A Practical Guide to Adoption for Family Lawyers' by Graham Pegg

'A Practical Guide to Industrial Disease Claims' by Andrew Mckie & Ian Skeate
'A Practical Guide to Conducting a Sheriff Court Proof' by Andrew Stevenson
'A Practical Guide to Vicarious Liability' by Mariel Irvine
'A Practical Guide to Applications for Landlord's Consent and Variation of Leases' by Mark Shelton
'A Practical Guide to Relief from Sanctions Post-Mitchell and Denton' by Peter Causton
'A Practical Guide to Equity Release for Advisors' by Paul Sams
'A Practical Guide to Financial Services Claims' by Chris Hegarty
'A Practical Guide to Financial Ombudsman Service Claims' by Adam Temple & Robert Scrivenor
'A Practical Guide to Running Housing Disrepair and Cavity Wall Claims – Second Edition' by Andrew Mckie & Ian Skeate
'A Practical Guide to Holiday Sickness Claims – Second Edition' by Andrew Mckie & Ian Skeate
'Arguments and Tactics for Personal Injury and Clinical Negligence Claims' by Dorian Williams
'A Practical Guide to Drone Law' by Rufus Ballaster, Andrew Firman, Eleanor Clot
'On Experts: CPR35 for Lawyers and Experts' by David Boyle
'An Introduction to Personal Injury Law' by David Boyle

www.ingramcontent.com/pod-product-compliance
Ingram Content Group UK Ltd.
Pitfield, Milton Keynes, MK11 3LW, UK
UKHW021239300926
15471UKWH00013B/767

9 781916 698895